Newman's Conveyancing Practice and Procedure

Fourmat Publishing

Lawyers Practice and Procedure Series

Newman's Conveyancing Practice and Procedure

by Vera D Gittins, LL.B, Solicitor

Consulting editor:
Phyllis E Newman, LL.B, M.Phil, Solicitor

London
Fourmat Publishing
1985

ISBN 0 906840 91 0

First published in two separate volumes as *Conveyancing of Freehold Property* (1980) and *Conveyancing of Leasehold Property* (1982).
This edition, 1985.

© 1985 Fourmat Publishing
27 & 28 St. Albans Place, Islington Green, London N1 0NX
Printed in Great Britain by Billing & Sons Ltd, Worcester

Foreword

Newman's Conveyancing Practice and Procedure presents Phyllis E Newman's admirable *Conveyancing of Freehold Property* (1980) and *Conveyancing of Leasehold Property* (1982) revised and incorporated in one volume. The various stages of conveyancing are explained in a logical sequence with emphasis on practice and procedure.

Efficient conveyancing demands accuracy, speed, and clear communication, and this book seeks to promote these aims. It is intended as a guide for newly-qualified solicitors, legal executives, and articled clerks, with limited experience in conveyancing.

VDG
June 1985

Contents

Table of cases

Table of statutes

Chapter 1

Taking instructions

1. Completing the instruction sheet

The only satisfactory way to take instructions is by personal interview. It is important to make notes in an efficient and businesslike manner so as to have a complete and accurate record of the client's requirements. To avoid the possibility of overlooking any necessary information it is wise to make notes on an instruction form either obtained from a law stationer, or prepared in the office and duplicated. It is preferable to have a form designed for use on the sale or purchase of freehold/leasehold, with a supplementary sheet for the grant of a new lease or underlease. See Appendix 1 for examples. Enter the details using black ink or black ballpoint as these photocopy well.

(a) The heading

agree completion date

It will assist later if you can readily check the preferred completion date, and whether the transaction is to be a concurrent sale and purchase. If both sale and purchase are involved, explain to your client the need to agree a completion date with both his purchaser and vendor and discuss whether he would be willing and able to obtain a bridging loan should this not be possible. Insert the client's name in block letters after the interview to assist filing.

(b) Particulars of the property

- Check the full address, if possible from the estate agent's particulars and note the price/premium.
- Note name and address of the local authority.
- Obtain a description of the property. This is important with regard to the grant or assignment of a lease of part(s) of a property such as a flat, or sale of part of a freehold.
- Ascertain who is in occupation and in what capacity.

- Is the sale or grant to be with vacant possession?
- If client is vendor check as far as possible his ownership, any third party interests, and whether the property is in mortgage.
- If client is granting a lease, check whether the freehold is in mortgage; if granting an underlease check whether the head lease or any intermediate lease is in mortgage.
- Ascertain the whereabouts of the title deeds, lease, and other documents relating to the property. If the deeds are held by a building society note the name, branch address, and roll number. If there is no subsisting mortgage the deeds may be held by a bank for safekeeping, in which case request client to write to the bank authorising release to your firm.

(c) Client

- Note full name(s) and check spelling.
- Ascertain marital status or relationship if property is, or is to be, jointly owned. Discuss the question of equitable ownership and explain. Spouses usually wish to hold as beneficial joint tenants but there may be good reason for them to hold as beneficial tenants in common. If they are to hold as tenants in common ascertain whether the beneficial entitlement will be in equal shares. This is an even more important consideration if the couple are not married. See *Bernard* v *Josephs* (1982), and D. G. Barnsley (1983) 127 SJ p.554.
- Obtain specimen signature(s) and ask client(s) to use this same signature on all documents. If client is a business firm or company ascertain who will sign documents. This will usually be the owner or company secretary.
- Telephone numbers (home and work) and full postal address including post code are important and may speed communication later.

(d) Other party

Record details and check that instructions have not been received to act for both parties to the transaction. Solicitors' Practice Rules 1936–1972 Rule 2 forbids acting for both vendor and purchaser with few exceptions.

(e) Estate agent

- If the client is vendor ask for details of the agreement entered into with the agent. Is there a sole agency or are there several agents involved?

- Check that the agency contract is in writing and contains no terms disadvantageous to your client. Warn against agreeing to an agent having sole selling rights.

- Ensure that commission will not be payable to more than one agent; will not be payable if completion does not take place; and that there will be no extra expenses, eg advertising.

- Advise the purchasing client to avoid paying a deposit to the estate agent; explain that this will not give him a contract. The agent is working for the vendor and is endeavouring to sell the property at maximum price as quickly as possible. The only service he might perform for the purchaser would be to obtain a mortgage offer in order to expedite the sale, and this may not be the best mortgage for the client's circumstances.

- A solicitor must be wary of having a new client referred to him by an estate agent. The Law Society have pointed out that there is a risk of breach of the Solicitors' Practice Rules 1936–1972 Rule 1.

(f) Survey arrangements

Check that the purchasing client is fully aware of the need for an independent survey. The vendor is normally under no duty to disclose physical defects, and the purchaser must satisfy himself as to the condition of the property before he is bound by contract.

For an old property, or if defects are suspected, eg in the roof, foundations, or in the drainage or electrical systems, a full structural survey by a qualified surveyor is essential. An unsatisfactory report may enable a reduced price to be negotiated, or will warn the client against proceeding with the purchase.

For an apparently sound property a "House Buyers' Report and Valuation" may be sufficient. The surveyor who undertakes this, a member of The Royal Institution of Chartered Surveyors, will inspect the visible and accessible parts of the property, and report on the condition, state of repair, and give an estimate of the market price.

With newly-built property reliance may perhaps be placed on the

3

National House-Building Council insurance scheme, the mortgagee's survey, and the local authority responsibility; see *Anns* v *Merton London Borough Council* (1978). A building society's survey alone cannot be relied on as the survey is little more than a valuation, but see *Yianni* v *Edwin Evans & Sons* (1982) regarding a possible duty of care owed by the surveyor to a purchaser as well as to the instructing mortgagee. If the surveyor acting for the building society also acts for your client, he may charge a reduced fee for the private survey.

(g) Financial arrangements

(i) Deposit — Enquire whether a deposit or reservation fee has already been paid. If so, how much, to whom, and on what basis?

Warn a vendor against accepting less than 10 per cent deposit or exchanging contracts until the full deposit has been received and, if paid by the purchaser's cheque, cleared by the bank. However, most forms of contract provide for payment by banker's draft or a cheque drawn on a solicitor's account.

Warn the purchaser that a deposit will be required a few days before contracts are exchanged.

(ii) Price — Note any agreements as to purchase price. Consider this in relation to the mortgage required as some building societies and banks charge differential rates of interest for larger loans. Consider also the price in relation to the stamp duty threshold.

(iii) Premium — Is a premium to be paid on the grant of the lease and, if so, how much?

(iv) Rent — Is rent to be paid, how much, and at what intervals? Will the rent include service and maintenance charges, and cover general and water rates, and sewerage charges?

If acting for a lessor, particularly of business premises, advise on the desirability of rent reviews and break clauses to allow for price inflation, and suggest suitable arrangements.

(v) Mortgage — If a purchaser will require a mortgage examine all the possibilities in the context of the client's and spouse's income, and the location, age, type and price of the property he is proposing to purchase, bearing in mind the tax position and family

responsibilities. The amount he will be able to borrow is unlikely to exceed 3 times the main income plus 1½ times any second income, and may possibly be limited to 80 per cent of the valuation of the property.

With a leasehold property, building societies and banks may not be willing to lend money for the purchase of a lease with less than 50 years unexpired, or which contains a term providing for forfeiture on bankruptcy of the tenant. Besides building societies and banks the mortgage field will include local authorities, insurance companies, and private lenders. In practice, for the purchaser of domestic property, the advice required will probably be confined to which building society is likely to be most helpful for this particular transaction, and whether the client's circumstances will be most benefitted by a repayment mortgage, or endowment mortgage linked to a life assurance policy, or a pension mortgage linked to a personal pension plan for a client who is self-employed or in non-pensionable employment.

If the client is a first-time purchaser of a lower-priced property enquire whether he would qualify for a home assistance loan under the Home Purchase Assistance and Housing Corporation Guarantee Act 1978.

If a purchaser is likely to require a bridging loan, warn that it should be so arranged that interest paid will qualify for tax relief.

If a vendor has contracted to lend the purchaser part of the price, to be secured by legal mortgage, pending completion he will have an equitable mortgage which requires protection as a land charge in unregistered title; by caution in registered title; or by registration under the Companies Act 1985 s.395 (previously s.95 of the 1948 Act) if created by a company. It has been held that an unpaid vendor's lien, resulting from a sale of land to a limited company does not require registration under s.395, but doubts have been expressed. The deposit of deeds by a company without a written memorandum to secure a debt does require registration under s.395.

If the vendor has a mortgage to be redeemed on completion, notice to the mortgagee will be required in accordance with the mortgage covenants. If there is a private mortgage six months' notice to redeem may be required, and the client will have to pay interest in lieu of notice for lesser time. Formal notice to redeem should be given at the earliest possible time, but if given before contracts have been exchanged and the sale does not proceed the client may be held to his notice.

(vi) Insurance — The purchaser may find an insurance or mortgage broker helpful, but should be advised to check whether a fee will

be charged, and to check also the broker's membership of a professional body. Registration is compulsory for insurance brokers under the Insurance Brokers (Registration) Act 1977, but not for mortgage brokers.

The purchaser with a dependent family, who chooses a repayment mortgage, should be advised to take out a mortgage protection policy to ensure that the loan will be repaid should he die during the term of the mortgage. The building society may insist on such a policy. Endowment mortgages will normally include life cover although there will be a choice of policy.

Explain to a purchaser that the property must be insured from the date of contract when the risk passes to him. Advise the client to insure to the full replacement value preferably with an index-linked policy, as the cost of rebuilding may be greater than the purchase price. If there is to be a building society mortgage the society may insist on arranging the insurance and will normally debit the premiums to the borrower's account. The society may insure from the date the acceptance of the offer is received; as soon as contracts have been exchanged; or may not insure until the advance is made at the completion of the purchase unless specially requested to do so beforehand. Carefully check the society's instructions or rules.

If a lease is being taken the terms may require insurance with a particular company, and the society should be made aware of this. If the insurance is provided by the lessor, eg a block policy for a building containing numerous flats, it will be necessary to check that the cover is acceptable to the building society.

In the case of a property in the course of erection special conditions may apply; some building societies will not insure until advised that the property is ready for occupation. In any case the insurer must be informed that the property is on a site where building operations are in progress. The vendor of an uncompleted building may have undertaken to keep the property insured until works are completed. Where the vendor has insured, check that the policy will be held for the benefit of the purchaser who will be the party at risk on exchange.

The vendor should be advised not to allow his insurance to lapse until completion as he will have to bear any loss should the purchaser successfully rescind the contract; see *Simmons* v *Pennington & Son* (1955).

(h) Fixtures

Note details of any agreement made between the parties with regard to carpets, curtains and runners, furniture, etc to be included in the purchase price or to be sold to the purchaser separately. Ask the vendor to supply a list of items to be included with the property, with an accurate description and their condition, and to indicate any fixtures and fittings not to be included in the sale. See *Hamp* v *Bygraves* (1983).

(i) Grant of lease or underlease

With the grant of a lease or underlease consider the question of costs and seek instructions. Where a long lease at a ground rent is being purchased for a capital consideration each party will pay his own costs, as in the purchase of freehold. The Costs of Leases Act 1958 provides similarly, but on the grant of a shorter lease it is usual to contract out of the Act by providing that the costs and disbursements of the landlord's solicitor and stamp duty on the lease and counterpart will be paid by the tenant. Any such arrangement must be made in advance in writing.

A lessee's solicitor should resist such an arrangement but, if the lessor insists, he should negotiate a definite figure rather than agree to pay the lessor's "proper costs" as these may be found to include such items as surveyor's fees.

Take specific and detailed instructions on rights, exceptions and reservations. If there is to be a lease of part or parts of a building, inform the client that a surveyor's detailed plan will be required and discuss arrangements for insurance, provision for repairs to the main fabric of the building, service and maintenance charges, and apportionment of general and water rates and sewerage charges, etc. Ascertain the present state of repair.

Advise the client on the effect of Landlord and Tenant legislation with regard to length of term, the amount of ground rent, implied obligations imposed on the lessor for repairs and maintenance of the building and equipment, the rights and remedies given to lessees in respect of such matters as contribution to maintenance funds and security of tenure.

Discuss provisions for terminating the lease.

In the case of a business lease consider whether there are any grounds for application to the Court to exclude the security of tenure provisions of the Landlord and Tenant Act 1954 s.38(4), as provided by the Law of Property Act 1969 s.5. If there are not, advise the client of the effect of legislation on the grant of a subtenancy. Consider also the advisability of limiting statutory compensation under s.37 of the 1954 Act.

The client may require advice as to the effect of a narrow user clause on the commercial value of the property.

(j) Preliminary enquiries

As far as possible obtain a vendor/lessor client's replies to a standard form of preliminary enquiries. Request him to supply any documents which he may hold such as receipts, guarantees, or maintenance agreements.

2. Conclusion of the interview

(a) Public Sector Housing

The Housing Act 1980 gives the right for certain tenants in the public sector to buy where the landlord owns the freehold. The right is to acquire the freehold of the house in which the tenant lives or, if he is the tenant of a flat, a lease of not less than 125 years at a rent not exceeding £10 per annum. The Act provides for a discount from the market value and gives the right to a mortgage to assist in the acquisition. The procedure, as laid down in the Act, is commenced by the tenant serving notice in the prescribed form on the landlord, claiming to exercise his right to buy. If acting for a client in this situation advise him of the requirements of the Act and the procedure. (Although the property is the purchaser's home, make the usual searches and enquiries paying particular attention to such matters as drainage, restrictions, facilities, services and service charges. Check that the amount of discount is correct and that the available mortgage is suitable for the purchaser.)

(b) Buying at auction

The client intending to bid at auction should be advised to consider having the property surveyed and obtaining an estimate for any repairs needed prior to the auction, particularly with an older property. Usually the vendor's solicitor will agree to reply to standard preliminary enquiries and, of course, the usual local authority searches and enquiries should also be made before the auction.

(c) Property subject to a tenancy

If the client is considering buying property occupied by a tenant, point out that there may be a "regulated tenancy" which can pass to another member of the tenant's family; the tenant may have no responsibility for repairs; and the rent, likely to be controlled, will be liable to tax. Full enquiries are essential.

(d) Client's financial situation

If the client is purchasing, discuss his financial situation in detail, including all expenses involved in moving into a property, eg search fees, survey fees, deposit, legal costs, mortgagee's costs, stamp duty, land registry fees, removal costs, insurance, and the possibility of a mortgage protection policy being called for by the building society, and VAT.

If a vendor is not purchasing another property concurrently ascertain whether he needs advice on investing the proceeds of the sale.

(e) Contract races

If instructions are given by a vendor to submit draft contracts to more than one prospective purchaser, whether simultaneously or otherwise, The Law Society directs that his solicitor (with his client's authority) must at once disclose and confirm in writing the vendor's decision direct to the solicitor acting for each prospective purchaser or, where no solicitor is acting, to the prospective purchaser(s) in person. If the vendor refuses to authorise disclosure the solicitor must cease acting for the vendor forthwith.

If a purchaser seems likely to become involved in a contract race, warn him of the risks in competing to purchase against time. In this situation the unsuccessful purchaser will have thrown away survey and search fees and costs; the successful may later regret a purchase made in haste.

(f) Concurrent transactions

Explain to the client the problems which may arise when the vendor is concurrently a purchaser. The sale and purchase will need to be kept strictly apart. Separate letters should be sent to the client in respect of each transaction, even though sent under the same cover. It is essential that every step is synchronised to ensure that exchange of contracts in both matters is simultaneous and the subsequent completions occur on the same day. If the client is depending on the money from the sale to pay for his purchase, failure to synchronise may cause him to require an expensive bridging loan. Add to this the "chain" situation usually involved in domestic conveyancing and the problems multiply. Although the solicitor is under pressure, care should be taken to keep the client fully informed so that he does not worry unduly and appreciates what is being done on his behalf.

(g) Leasehold obligations

If relevant, advise a lessee or assignee on the nature and extent of leasehold obligations or, if acting for the assignor, on the obligations attendant on assignment.

(h) References

If references will be required ask the client to supply the name and address of business, bank, and if necessary personal, referees. Where an assignment to a limited company is sought, it has been held unreasonable, unless the lease expressly so provides, to require personal guarantees from the company directors.

(i) Subject to contract

Explain that the transaction will be "subject to contract", or on the grant of a lease if there is to be no contract "subject to lease", normally enabling either party to withdraw until contracts or lease and counterpart are exchanged.

3. Action immediately after interview

Write to the client — Set out his instructions in detail, including the terms of any undertaking he has authorised, to avoid misunderstanding. Draw attention again to the nature and extent of the client's obligations in relation to the transaction (Appendix 2, Letters V1, P1).

To a lessee client, set out the terms he requires in the lease and pay particular attention to any special requirements, eg if a residence is to be used partly for business or professional purposes, or if there is to be industrial user.

To a lessor client, outline the terms of the proposed lease or underlease in accordance with his instructions; ensure that all points are adequately covered.

Write to the solicitor acting for other party — head all correspondence "subject to contract" or "subject to lease" in order to avoid it being held that a contract has been concluded; see *Tiverton Estates Ltd* v *Wearwell Ltd* (1975) (Appendix 2, letters V2, P2). Such words as "subject to contract" once used will continue to apply throughout the negotiations until agreement is reached. However, take care not to inadvertently waive the "subject to contract" qualification; see *Griffiths* v *Young* (1970). If acting for a purchaser or lessee, request a draft contract, copy of the lease, or draft lease, as appropriate. State the vendor's/lessor's name, the address of the property, the purchase price, and main features of a proposed lease.

Write to the estate agent — Confirm the terms of the agency contract for the vendor; ensure that the agent has no authority to make any statements on behalf of the vendor; and ensure that any deposit will be paid to the solicitor acting for the vendor/lessor, not to the agent.

Obtain a copy of the agent's circular giving particulars of the property as this will be helpful whether acting for either vendor or purchaser. (Appendix 2, Letters V4, P3).

If acting for a vendor or lessor request the title deeds, or Land or Charge Certificate if the property has registered title. If obtaining these from a mortgagee quote the roll number or reference and mention the proposed sale. An undertaking will be required and thereafter your failure to honour this may be regarded as a breach of professional conduct (Appendix 2, Letter V3). Mark the file clearly to avoid the possibility of the undertaking being overlooked at a later stage. If completing a bank's standard form of undertaking ensure that the terms are not unnecessarily wide and the requirement for payment to the bank agrees with your client's instructions. If necessary amend the form.

The Law Society will not imply into an undertaking to pay money out of the proceeds of the sale of property, a term that the undertaking is intended to take effect "only if the proceeds of the sale actually come into the hands of the solicitor giving the undertaking"; see *Guide to Professional Conduct* p.69. The solicitor should make clear in the undertaking that it is to take effect if the proceeds of sale come into his hands and are available. The Law Society also suggests that the solicitor should expressly insert any necessary term to disclaim personal liability. However, in *R* v *Wooding* (1978) a term in an undertaking excluding personal liability was held to be evidence that the solicitor must have been aware of his client's fraudulent intentions, and the solicitor was held criminally liable. If a client, especially a business client, is not well known to you consider the danger of giving an undertaking which may be used to obtain an advance from a bank in a sham transaction.

If the title to the property is registered, apply to the appropriate district land registry, once the title number is known, to obtain office copies of the entries on the Register and filed plan (Form A44).

The sale of freehold property and assignment of an existing lease or underlease is continued at Chapter 2.

The grant of new lease or underlease is continued at Chapter 4.

Chapter 2

The contract

1. Check title deeds

When the vendor's solicitor has obtained the title deeds or, if the title is registered, the land or charge certificate, these should be examined paying particular attention to the following:

(a) Sale of freehold

Ascertain that your client is the owner, that there are no third party interests and no impediments to the proposed sale. Check for restrictive covenants.

(b) Assignment of lease or underlease

Check the assignment or grant to the vendor and any dealings.

Check the lease and any superior lease for restrictions particularly on assignment and change of use. A covenant against parting with possession will preclude assignment; see *Marks* v *Warren* (1979).

Check the lease as to requirements for the lessor's consent and make the necessary application. Consent can be in simple form but should be signed by the person giving consent, not his solicitor or agent.

If there is to be assignment of part only of the property comprised in a lease there will have to be apportionment of the rent and this may be ground for refusal of consent by a superior lessor. If this is not acceptable the vendor may remain liable for the whole of the rent. The Law Society's Contract for Sale includes provision for rescission in the event that consent to assign from a superior lessor is not forthcoming.

Apply for any references required by the lessor as soon as possible. It may be necessary to obtain a bank reference, a personal reference, and a business reference in respect of the proposed assignee; this is more common with business leases than residential leases.

Investigate the credentials of the proposed assignee carefully and make a search in the Companies Register where appropriate. It is important for the assignor as well as the lessor to have a reliable assignee who will not default on the covenants in the lease.

Check the lessor's covenants and obligations in any underlease.

Investigate the position between the client and anyone having superior title for disputes or pending claims.

2. Draft contract

When the title deeds have been checked the vendor's solicitor must prepare in duplicate the draft contract for the sale or assignment to be sent to the purchaser's solicitor for approval. This may be typed on a plain sheet of paper, but it is usual and preferable to use the latest edition of a recognised standard form such as The Law Society's Contract for Sale or the National Conditions of Sale. Both are four-page forms obtainable from law stationers. (Conveyancing forms are listed in Appendix 3).

Page 1 requires details of the parties to the contract, particulars of the property, the purchase price, and the deposit.

Pages 2 and 3 contain the General Conditions of Sale that are to form part of the contract. The vendor's solicitor must have a thorough knowledge of the General Conditions on the different standard forms, as they vary. The choice of form should be dictated by whichever conditions provide maximum protection in the particular circumstances of the sale. Any General Condition may be excluded, modified, or replaced by a Special Condition.

Page 4 contains the Special Conditions. Every contract will have conditions that are common to other contracts and can be covered by General Conditions, but invariably some conditions will be unique to this particular transaction, and the vendor's solicitor must strive to meet exactly his client's requirements.

(a) Parties

The names of the vendor(s) and purchaser(s) must be correct. If unsure of the purchaser's name and address, leave a space for his solicitor to insert them. Check that the name of the vendor on the title deeds, or on the copy entries for a registered title, agrees with that given at your initial interview. Check also from the deeds that the vendor is the person solely entitled to sell and convey the land or, if not, that any requisite party is compellable, otherwise the purchaser will be able to rescind even though the other party is willing to join in the conveyance. Preferably bind all necessary parties to the conveyance by making them parties to the contract.

(b) Particulars of the property

The property must be described accurately, leaving no room for doubt. With an assignment, details of the lease must be given, and a copy supplied. If the title is registered the description can follow that contained in the property register, making reference also to the title number and filed plan. If the title is less than absolute this must be stated.

If the title is unregistered do not simply repeat the description as it appeared in the conveyance to the vendor but first enquire whether any changes have made this inaccurate, and check also the description in earlier documents of title.

Include in the description any rights or restrictions which adversely affect or which benefit the land, such as restrictive covenants or easements.

Check whether the property requires to be identified in the contract by reference to a plan. If so, check the accuracy of any plan already on the deeds before you use this, and ascertain that there has been no alteration to the boundaries shown. Depending on title, the property can be described, "as delineated on the plan" or, "as shown on the plan for the purpose of identification only". Do not use both, or other similarly conflicting terms together.

If the vendor is selling part of his land, whether his title is registered or unregistered, it is essential to have the contract plan prepared by a qualified surveyor.

(c) Deposit

Insert the amount of deposit; not less than 10 per cent of the purchase price to be paid by the purchaser.

Although there is no requirement at common law for payment of a deposit, provision for a deposit on a freehold sale, or an assignment of a lease for a premium, should be made an express term of the contract and the receipt for the deposit paid should be included in the contract.

The deposit should be required to be paid to the vendor's solicitor on exchange of contracts as is usually provided for in the General Conditions, and not to the estate agent. The proper provision is for the deposit to be held by the vendor's solicitor as stakeholder, unless the vendor is selling in a fiduciary capacity when it should be held as agent for the vendor.

Property developers and builders frequently require the deposit to be held by their solicitor as agent and not as stakeholder so that they can use the money before completion of the sale to finance their operations.

Pressure is also put on solicitors by clients who wish to use the deposit on their sale as the deposit on their purchase. If the purchaser agrees he may wish to secure the position by taking an equitable charge on the vendor's property.

(d) Interest rate

The standard form contracts make provision for a contract rate of interest although interest is often quoted by reference to a clearing bank's base rate. It is necessary to increase the rate above this if the vendor is to receive an acceptable market rate. Ensure that the rate on the sale contract is high enough to cover the interest on a bridging loan should this be required by the vendor, and ensure that the rate is not lower than the rate included in his own purchase contract.

(e) Completion date

The completion date is a matter for careful negotiation between the parties, bearing in mind that the standard forms of contract will supply a date if no date or a wrong date is inserted, and will also import a time.

If the vendor is a builder he may wish to fix a date too soon after completion of the erection of the building. It may be necessary to point out to such a client that the purchaser must be given reasonable time for a surveyor's inspection and report, and for the building society's advance to be obtained.

It is advisable to keep a date in mind that would possibly be acceptable to both sides but this should not be inserted until a final agreement has been reached just before exchange.

If your client is both selling and purchasing and wishes the transactions to be completed on the same day then agreement of the parties on both sides must be obtained.

There is a risk that completion "on or before" a certain date may be construed as making time of the essence when not so intended. This phrase is better avoided and a specific date should be inserted.

If the vendor wishes time to be of the essence this will have to be made a term of the contract, except where it is so by implication, eg on the sale of certain types of commercial property. The vendor should be advised that this provision can be a two-edged sword.

(f) Vacant possession

This usually implies vacant possession of the whole of the property, legally and physically. The contract should provide for vacant possession on completion unless the property is being sold or assigned subject to occupation by a tenant, in which case the contract should give details of any lease, tenancy or agreement, and completion will give only the right to receive rent.

If for any other reason vacant possession is not being given immediately on completion, or if the purchaser is to be allowed into occupation prior to completion, a special condition should be inserted in the contract, and matters such as occupier's liability and insurance dealt with.

There are terms dealing with occupation prior to completion in most standard forms of contract but they may not be sufficient for the particular situation.

In the case of business property a clause in respect of possession prior to completion will need to be comprehensive to cover stock and assets, profits, loss, tax liabilities, etc.

Remember that vacant possession as a contract term does not merge in the conveyance.

(g) Restrictive covenants

The vendor must fully reveal in the contract every restriction, easement or reservation affecting the property which will bind the purchaser.

If the title is unregistered check that post-1925 negative covenants have been registered at the Land Charges Registry; if pre-1926 they will bind because of the doctrine of notice. If the title is registered reference can be made to the relevant register entries.

Check whether the vendor will remain personally liable on the covenants after the sale and, if so, a covenant to observe, perform, and indemnify will be required of the purchaser and, on the latter point check the General Conditions in the particular form of contract used.

Where there is to be an assignment for valuable consideration of an existing lease the Law of Property Act 1925 s.77(1)(c) will imply a covenant by the assignee, or joint or several covenants by the assignees (if more than one) with the assignor for the residue of the leasehold term to duly pay the rent, observe and perform the covenants and conditions and indemnify the assignor. Rather than relying on this implied covenant an express clause should be inserted that the assignee will indemnify the assignor against all claims for breach of the lessee's covenants under the lease and the contract should state that such express covenant will be required. The vendor is not entitled to such unless he is the original lessee or is under a similar obligation.

(h) New obligations

Check instructions on the imposition of new restrictive or positive covenants and the reservation or grant of rights and easements. If the vendor is selling only part of his land it is vital to inspect the property to see what rights must be reserved and obligations imposed. In particular, note the rights he will require for access, pipes, wires, and cables. Amenity may require the imposition of new covenants on the land being sold, eg to fence. Guard against the effect of the rule in *Wheeldon* v *Burrows* (1879), and the Law of Property Act 1925 s.62.

(i) Capacity

Check the title deeds to ascertain how the vendor holds the property, eg as beneficial owner or trustee, and insert this as the capacity in which he will convey. Keep in mind the covenants for title which will be implied by the Law of Property Act 1925 s.76. An assignment of a lease as "beneficial owner" will imply that the rent has been paid to the date of the assignment and the covenants in the lease have been performed, so that if repairing covenants have not been fulfilled even though the assignee has agreed to take the property in its present condition, the assignment should expressly negative such implied covenants. The Law Society's Contract for Sale (1984) clause 8(5) provides for this.

(j) Title

If the title is unregistered check whether it is necessary to employ the same root as that given when the vendor acquired the land, or whether there is a later deed which proves ownership of the legal estate, identifies the land, and deals with the equitable interests. If a shorter period than the statutory fifteen years is being offered the purchaser will be entitled to assume that the document from which the title commences deals with a transaction where title was fully investigated, eg is not a voluntary conveyance, so it is essential to state the nature of the dealing.

If the title is registered the Land Registration Act 1925 s.110(1) requires the following to be provided:

(i)   authority to inspect the register;

(ii)   office copy of subsisting entries in the register;

(iii) office copy of any filed plans;

(iv) copies or abstracts of any documents or any part thereof noted on the register so far as they affect the land to be sold (except charges or incumbrances which are to be discharged or overridden at, or prior to, completion).

If the title is less than absolute, ie possessory or qualified, the purchaser will need to investigate the pre-registration title as in unregistered conveyancing. If the vendor is unable to provide proof of prior title, this will have to be made a term of the contract so that the purchaser is made aware of the risk at the pre-contract stage. The same applies where the register refers to the contents of a document of which no copy was available on first registration.

(k) Special terms

Any special term for which the purchaser may have asked to accommodate his particular circumstances, eg "subject to obtaining a satisfactory mortgage", "subject to survey", "subject to the purchaser obtaining planning permission", needs careful drafting if the term is not to render the contract void for uncertainty.

(l) Management company

On assignment of a lease which requires the lessee to be a member of a management company provision should be made in the contract for the assignee to purchase the share from the vendor, usually for a nominal sum.

(m) Furniture and fittings

If furniture and fittings are to be included in the sale, there should be a separate allocation of price to these items and an inventory attached to the contract.

(n) Building estates

A standard contract for the sale of plots on a building estate with houses to be erected thereon, needs to be drawn so that it can serve with minor adaptations for each plot. Incorporate a standard form conveyance or transfer which includes reference to ownership of boundaries, reservation and granting of easements, and restrictive and positive covenants. Every contract should be accompanied by:

(i) documentation as to the vendor's title;
(ii) a copy of any agreement with the local authority for making-up roads and footpaths, and the supporting bond;
(iii) replies to the standard long form of preliminary enquiries.

If the development land has unregistered title it should be voluntarily registered, which can be done if there are twenty or more house plots or a like number of purpose-built flats to be erected. When the site layout plan has been approved by the Land Registry, extracts from it can be used in conjunction with contracts and transfers as well as for the purpose of official searches. It should be indicated that the vendor will not permit amendments to be made by the purchaser's solicitor except by way of deleting alternative clauses, eg whether or not a joint tenancy clause is required.

(o) Sale by auction

A contract for sale by auction will contain Special and General Conditions, the latter usually incorporated by reference to standard form conditions. Copies of these standard form conditions should be circulated with the particulars. It would be helpful to make available up-to-date replies to local searches and enquiries to prospective purchasers before auction.

It is important to make the sale subject to a reserve price, and this fact must be stated in the particulars or conditions to comply with the Sale of Land by Auction Act 1867 s.5.

The vendor's solicitor should attend the auction to answer enquiries but the contract, which is normally exchanged immediately after the auction, should be signed on the vendor's behalf by the auctioneer, as the auctioneer not the solicitor, is the vendor's agent to conclude the sale.

3. Checklist

Ensure that:

● all names and addresses in the contract are complete and correctly spelled;

- the property is incontrovertibly identified;
- any plan used has been checked against the particulars;
- the vendor has excepted and reserved any rights he may need over retained land, common parts of the building, car parks, or gardens, etc;
- the vendor is not by implication passing any rights he does not intend to give;
- all incumbrances and latent defects have been fully disclosed, bearing in mind the Misrepresentation Act 1967 and the Law of Property Act 1969 s.24(1), as to land charges;
- a viable root of title has been provided which can be proved with connecting ownership to the vendor's title, and all necessary documentation for proof is in hand or available;
- the vendor has been given sufficient protection against all possible liabilities after parting with the property, eg that the purchaser shall assume that all covenants have been observed and will give an appropriate indemnity or, where there is some slight deficiency in title, that the purchaser is required to accept this;
- any required consents to the transaction have been received or will be to hand before exchange of contracts;
- the conditions in the contract conform with client's instructions and he has confirmed the purchase price, deposit, and any other payments — take care with fixtures and fittings which are not to be included in the sale.

4. Despatching the draft contract

After checking the draft contract send two copies to the purchaser's solicitor for his approval. Attach to each contract a copy of any deed, plan, restrictive covenant or inventory referred to in the draft and a copy of the lease if assigning. If the title is registered send also Land Registry "office copies" of entries on the register and the filed plan; photocopies will not be adequate. If the Register entries reveal a purchase price, a practice now discontinued by the Land Registry, and the vendor does not wish this to be disclosed, the whole of the proprietorship register should be withheld until exchange of contracts. The Law Society have disapproved of cutting out the price from the page (Appendix 2, Letter V5).

5. Replies to preliminary enquiries

If the transaction is to be a hurried one a standard long form of enquiries before contract can be sent with the draft contract, complete with replies which have been carefully checked with the vendor to ensure that they are true and accurate. Standard form enquiries with replies should always be sent with the draft contract and all relevant documentation, when newly-erected properties are being sold on a developer's estate.

Later, the purchaser's solicitor will usually make his own enquiries on matters arising from the contract. The vendor's solicitor should avoid the too common practice of giving merely cursory or ritual replies to preliminary enquiries. Proper information will assist the transaction. Most of the necessary information should have been obtained when taking instructions from the vendor and this can now be supplemented by copies of planning permissions, National House Building Council agreements and certificates, etc which should be with the title deeds (Appendix 2, Letters V6, V7).

Responsibility for the accuracy of replies to preliminary enquiries, and later to requisitions on title, should be that of the vendor and not his solicitor.

Replies are representations only but can amount to a misrepresentation or negligent misstatement of fact, particularly where the vendor has or should have special information. Silence does not normally constitute misrepresentation, and the maxim *caveat emptor* applies unless the Misrepresentation Act 1967 protects the purchaser. The vendor has a duty to inform the purchaser of subsequent changes to pre-contract replies.

Conditions in a contract restricting the liability of the vendor for statements made, may not protect him if the provisions of the Misrepresentation Act 1967 or the Unfair Contract Terms Act 1977 apply.

In equity a purchaser may rescind where he has been induced to enter into the contract by a false statement of fact made by the vendor.

Chapter 3

The contract: approval and exchange

On receipt of the draft contract the purchaser's solicitor should check carefully to ensure that it is a sound contract and, as far as possible, meets the requirements of his client (Appendix 2, Letter P4).

Consider the following points:

1. Title

(a) Sale of freehold

If the land needs to be identified by reference to a plan, ensure that a plan is referred to in the contract so that it can be included in the conveyance, otherwise the purchaser may not be allowed a plan, even though provided at his own expense, unless he pays the cost of the vendor's surveyor to check it.

The vendor must show he is selling the land in fee simple absolute in possession free from all incumbrances except those subject to which the contract is expressed to be made.

Check the root of title to be supplied is impeccable and preferably provides more than the statutory fifteen year period. Twenty years will provide the benefit of the Law of Property Act 1925 s.45(6) on recitals. If the root is an assent by personal representatives, stipulate that the Probate or Letters of Administration shall be produced.

If the title is registered, the vendor is holding out that he is the registered proprietor with absolute title selling free from entries on the register and over-riding interests, except those which the contract expressly includes.

An express representation as to title can be relied on by the purchaser and it has been held that it is no defence to the vendor that had the purchaser investigated he could have discovered the facts to be otherwise.

(b) Assignment of lease or underlease

Check the General and Special Conditions in the contract concerning title.

The Law of Property Act 1925 s.44, as amended, will give only a right to production of the lease and all assignments under which it has been held for the previous fifteen years.

Unless the lease is registered with absolute leasehold title ask for the reversionary title to be deduced. If the assignor cannot produce an abstracted title a clause should be required in the contract that if there appear to be restrictions or liabilities prejudicially affecting the leasehold interest the assignee may rescind.

Copies of all counterpart leases or agreements with underlessees must be produced as part of the title, and enquiries should be made regarding any restrictions which will become binding on the purchaser and any mortgagee.

Where the building contains only two flats or maisonettes the original freehold owner may have divested himself of all interest in the property. If so, the lessee of each flat should possess the counterpart lease of the other flat, and there should be corresponding mutual covenants.

2. Incumbrances

Check that restrictive covenants are enforceable and that the vendor is properly entitled to any indemnity covenant he is requiring in the contract.

Check that the client is fully aware of the effect of old or new restrictive covenants to be imposed and all rights and easements subject to which the property is being sold.

If old restrictive covenants would impede the purchaser's plans, examine the possibility of an indemnity insurance policy. If the covenants are likely to be enforceable, examine the grounds and the likely cost of an application to the Lands Tribunal for removal or modification of the covenants. If such an application is to be made planning permission for the proposed development should be first obtained.

With an assignment check carefully the clauses in the lease, note particularly any of an unusual nature. Advise the client immediately if they appear unduly onerous or conflict with his interests. See *Sykes* v *Midland Bank Executor and Trustee Co Ltd* (1971).

Check the lease with regard to restrictions on assignment and whether consent or licence to assign is required from the vendor's lessor or from any superior lessor. If required, has an approach

been made and with what result? Do not proceed until the necessa,
consent is produced, unless the assignor agrees to be responsible fo.
the assignee's legal costs if the assignor cannot proceed.

3. Deposit

Check that the deposit is not more than 10 per cent of the purchase
price, and is to be held by the vendor's solicitor as stakeholder. If the
vendor's solicitor insists on holding the deposit as agent and the
vendor is neither a builder nor in a fiduciary capacity, consider
asking the vendor to give an equitable charge over his property. See
The Conveyancer and Property Lawyer Precedents, page 1826. The
charge will require registration as a C(iii) Land Charge in
unregistered title, or by way of caution in registered title.

4. Special conditions

Check the effect of any special conditions designed to exclude or
modify a standard contract condition, eg reduction of the period of
notice to make time of the essence, and warn the client accordingly.

The contract may contain a term limiting the purchaser's right to
investigate the title fully or stating that the property is sold subject
to any general incumbrances. A standard term in most contracts is
that any error or omission in the particulars shall not annul the sale.
There are numerous cases where the vendor has been unable to
enforce the contract, despite the inclusion of such a condition, for a
purchaser must not be misled and the vendor must disclose defects
of title of which he knows or ought to know. Nevertheless, the
purchaser's solicitor must be wary of accepting limitations on his
right of investigation. It may be held that the purchaser had
knowledge of incumbrances or defects and impliedly contracted to
accept a title made subject to them.

A condition requiring the purchaser to assume a certain situation, eg
that all covenants have been observed, will not bind a purchaser if
the vendor knew or ought to have known that the statement was
untrue, or if he did not believe it to be true.

If the contract is on a standard form, it should be considered
whether any clauses need amending, eg in The Law Society's
General Conditions of Sale (1984), Clauses 6(3) and 8(5) may not be
acceptable.

If the purchaser intends to carry out any construction work or
change of use, planning permission should be obtained prior to
contract, or the contract made subject to it being obtained. Extreme
care is necessary in the wording of such condition.

5. Preliminary enquiries

The vendor is under no duty to disclose patent defects, and not even latent defects unless of such a nature that they would prevent the use or enjoyment of the land for the purpose for which the vendor is contracting to sell or knows it is being purchased.

After carefully checking the draft contract and any documents included, prepare the list of enquiries to be asked of the vendor before contract.

Many firms of solicitors have their own form of preliminary enquiries but often these are repetitious and not well drawn. A standard form available from law stationers is adequate; additional enquiries relevant to the particular property and the terms of the draft contract can be appended and irrelevant enquiries should be deleted. It is poor conveyancing practice to send inappropriate enquiries. Common courtesy will require the enquiries to be sent in duplicate (Appendix 2, Letter P5).

Before framing preliminary enquiries the purchaser's solicitor should visit the property so that he is aware of the area and potential development threats, the age of the property and of subsequent additions, means of access, need for easements, demarcation of boundaries, ownership of walls and fences, and patent rights of other parties or of the public. It may be necessary to check measurements, eg of the frontage or of access to a garage.

In the purchase of a building under construction, require production of the specification. Examine the agreement between the developer and the local authority regarding roads and footpaths, and the supporting bond.

Specific enquiry should be made to ascertain whether anyone may have an overriding interest due to occupation or contribution towards the cost of the property; see *Williams & Glyn's Bank Ltd* v *Boland* (1980).

Unless the property is being sold for use for a defined purpose, responsibility lies on the purchaser to ascertain that the land can be used for the purpose he has in mind. He will need to raise planning enquiries with both the vendor and the local planning authority. It has been held that there is no implied obligation on the vendor to disclose general restrictions on the permitted user. The matter is of particular importance in business user and in such a case it is advised that planning enquiries be made back to 1948; even though it may be too late for an enforcement notice to be served in respect of unlawful development, the use will not become lawful and available. See *LTSS Print and Supply Services Ltd* v *Hackney London Borough Council (1976)*.

In usual matters it will be necessary to make enquiries back to December 1963, the date of limit on challenge by way of enforcement notice in most areas.

Purchasers of commercial property are particularly susceptible to liability for heavy rating surcharge where property is unused. An enquiry should be made of the vendor regarding any period of non-user; if necessary a clause should be required in the contract whereby the vendor undertakes appropriate liability. Generally, standard form conditions do not protect the purchaser in this respect.

Enquiries on assignment of lease or underlease

For a purchaser, even though the vendor may remain liable on the covenants, the only safe assumption is that he will not be available to meet claims for matters subsequently discovered. The purchaser's solicitor must make every effort to ascertain the position by preliminary enquiries.

Confirm that the original lease or underlease will be handed over on completion, even though the title is registered. If the lease is not the headlease request copies of all superior leases.

Ascertain whether there have been any deeds of variation; if so request copies.

Request copies of all deeds and documents including insurance policies containing terms which the lessee will have to covenant to observe. Enquire whether all the lessee's covenants in all documents have been duly observed and performed.

Ascertain whether there are any restrictive covenants registered against the reversion. Have they been observed? Has the vendor received any intimation of a possible claim? In *White* v *Bijou Mansions Ltd* (1938), the lessee was bound by restrictive covenants registered against the freehold title although unable to discover them.

Check whether there is a mortgage or charge on any superior lease which excludes the statutory power of leasing. If so, has the mortgagee consented to the grant of an inferior lease including the lease now to be sold?

Enquire into the state of repair and, if the tenant is responsible, check that repairing covenants have been observed. Check maintenance accounts and other outgoings for the last three years at least.

The purchaser may be taking an assignment of property, part of which is sublet, so that he will become landlord of that part. Request copies of all counterpart leases or agreements with any subtenant; these must be produced as part of the title and handed over on completion. Full enquiries should be made as to any restrictions which will become binding on the purchaser or his mortgagee.

(i) Make full enquiry as to each subtenant; his rent, and whether a rent has been registered.

(ii) Ascertain whether there are arrears of rent owing.

(iii) Enquire as to repairs, including any claims against the landlord made by a subtenant for repairs to be done which may become the subject matter of an action.

(iv) If the subtenant is in default and it is possible to serve notice to quit, the vendor must be required to do this and to bring necessary proceedings to enforce it. The purchaser must avoid involvement in the claims and counterclaims of such an action.

Ensure that the contract deals equitably with apportionments. Obtain copies of accounts for expenditure on the upkeep of the buildings. Check specifically the position on the last year's maintenance charges as to whether they have been assessed and paid. If they have not, it will have to be determined how the liability is to be assessed.

Problems may arise with apportionment of rent and other outgoings if there is a long delay between contract and completion. In the interval large sums may have been expended on repairs, perhaps under pressure from the local authority. The purchaser's solicitor should make enquiries and estimate any forthcoming demands which could affect his client. The purchaser may be taking on an unknown liability, and the vendor may not be available when the account is delivered. There may need to be security offered by the vendor, or some part of the purchase price withheld, or a deposit held in a joint bank account by the solicitors for the vendor and purchaser.

6. Local searches and enquiries

Whether title to the land is registered or unregistered, a requisition for search and a form of enquiries should be sent to the appropriate local authority. The applicant must be familiar with the questions and be aware of their significance otherwise the replies will be meaningless. Replies to searches and enquiries made by the vendor's solicitor and handed over with the draft contract can be accepted as the Local Land Charges Act 1975 s.10 provides for compensation to a purchaser for the local authority's failure to register or disclose a charge, and liability for a negligent reply to an enquiry. Generally, it is preferable for the purchaser's solicitor to make his own searches and enquiries and to repeat them if there is delay in completing the purchase.

Both search and enquiries are made on standard forms; each must be submitted in duplicate together with plans, if required to identify the land, and with the appropriate fee.

The standard form of enquiries varies according to the location of the land; one form for district councils, and a slightly different form for London borough councils. The enquiries are set out in two parts. All enquiries in Part I will be answered for the basic fee and cover such vital matters as roads, drainage, and planning. Part II questions will only be answered if specifically requested and on payment of an additional fee. Supplementary questions can be added on the same basis. It is essential that all relevant enquiries for the particular property are made. It is also necessary to bear in mind that proposed development on an adjoining site and adjacent area will not be revealed unless specific enquiry is made, yet such development could make the proposed purchase undesirable or uneconomic.

The requisition (Form LLC1) is for an official search of the local land charges register. The register is divided into twelve numbered parts and it is usual to apply for a search of the whole register. The official certificate of search is important in that it may reveal matters which do not require disclosure by the vendor, although it gives no priority or protection against future registrations.

Depending on the property, particular attention may be necessary as to liability for road works. When the property is situated in a new development the agreement and supporting bond arranged with the local authority must be examined, copies being required from the vendor's solicitor. It is important to ascertain that payment by, or security being provided by, the vendor in respect of making-up roads and footpaths is adequate, especially if there is likely to be delay and rising costs. The purchaser's solicitor should require a clause in the contract that road works will be carried out to the satisfaction of the local authority and so maintained until taken over by the local authority. Preferably there should be a term for retention of part of the purchase money if the works are not finished on completion of the purchase. Depending on the area, particular attention may need to be directed to the local authority's slum clearance schemes, and improvement areas.

If the purchaser wishes to develop the land he would be well advised to apply for outline planning permission before exchange of contracts. Check carefully the terms of any planning permission previously granted and any conditions attached thereto.

7. Other searches and enquiries

(a) Unregistered title

Index Map search: Where the land has unregistered title it is essential to make a search of the public index map and parcels index. Application for an official search is made to the district land registry for the area (Land Registry Form 96). A plan of the property will be necessary unless the area is one of compulsory registration and the property can be identified by a street number. The plan must contain sufficient detail to enable the land to be identified on the Ordnance Survey map. The search will reveal whether the land is registered or affected by any caution against first registration or a priority notice.

Land Charges Registry searches: It was customary to require the vendor's solicitor to supply sufficient information for searches against the names of all owners back to 1 January 1926, and The Law Society advised that such searches should be made prior to contract. However, by the Law of Property Act 1969 s.24(1), a purchaser's knowledge of a registered charge is now determined by his "actual knowledge" at the time of the contract; this includes imputed knowledge, eg from a solicitor or agent acting in the transaction. Authorities differ as to whether Land Charges Registry searches should still be made prior to contract, the better opinion is that such searches should be so made. If a purchaser discovers a registered incumbrance which cannot be removed, a right of rescission may not be helpful if he has already contracted concurrently to sell his own property. In any case, early discovery of an incumbrance will avoid delay later. Moreover, if the vendor is bankrupt the sooner the proposed purchaser discovers this fact, the better.

In theory searches should be made back to 1 January 1926, but there is State compensation if the full fifteen years statutory period has been searched without revealing an incumbrance which is subsequently found to bind the purchaser. The difficulty in practice is to obtain sufficient information from the vendor's solicitor before contract to make searches against the names of all estate owners in respect of whom there are no clear certificates with the title deeds. However, the vendor's solicitor should co-operate for the purchaser may well prefer not to purchase a property with an incumbrance, and may not regard compensation as sufficient recompense. A fresh search will have to be made against the vendor before completion in order to ensure priority.

(b) Registered title

If the title is registered, in theory no search of the Land Charges Register is necessary. However, if the title registered is not absolute but possessory or qualified, then searches need to be made as though the land had unregistered title. Here a risk may have to be taken for the nature of the title usually connotes lack of available information. Thus searches should be made in time for the purchaser to consider whether or not he would be wise to enter into the contract.

(c) In all cases

Commons Registration search: Where the land has never been built on, a search in the Registers of Common Land and Town or Village Greens should be made. This will reveal whether the land is registered as such or whether there are common rights over any part. This applies whether the title is unregistered or registered. A requisition form for an official search (Form CR21) will be supplied by the County Council or is obtainable from law stationers. It has been held to be negligence for a solicitor to fail to make such a search unless the property was sited in a densely built-up area, even though the registration had been improperly made and was subsequently vacated; see *G & K Ladenbau (UK) Ltd* v *Crawley & de Reya* (1978). The search should be made at an early stage before contract as the vendor may not be aware of the registration.

Countryside: Enquiries should be made at the same time as the local land charges search regarding access agreements or orders made under the National Parks and Access to the Countryside Act 1949, and agreements between the landowner and the Countryside Commission or the local authority under the Countryside Act 1968, for a purchaser will take subject to them.

Trees: Tree Preservation Orders are made under planning legislation by the district council and should be revealed in the local authority search. Forestry dedication covenants under the Forestry Act 1967 are thought to be registrable as restrictive covenants. Licences for felling trees under the 1967 Act and the Trees Act 1970 often contain conditions enforceable against the owner of the land and thus are a burden on the land which the vendor has a duty to disclose.

Enclosure awards: On the purchase of rural land enquiries should be made of the county council as to enclosure awards, as these may reveal the existence of rights of way or public rights over the land.

Wayleave orders: The existence of a wayleave order in connection with an oil pipeline or works accessory thereto is registrable in the local land charges register. The effect is serious in that it can prevent any development by way of building, excavation or deposit of materials, and even some farming operations.

Areas of Outstanding Natural Beauty: If local authority searches and enquiries reveal that the property is situated in such an area, or in a Green Belt, the client should be warned that there is little prospect of permission being obtained for any development.

Railway fencing: Where land abuts on a railway an official search can be made as to responsibility for maintenance of fences. Application should be made to the Regional Estate Surveyor for the appropriate British Rail Region.

Sewers: Enquiries as to potential sewerage liabilities are affected by the Water Act 1973 by which sewerage functions were transferred to regional water authorities, and the local authority may be unable to give replies as to resolutions. In such cases enquiry will have to be made of the regional water authority. Where the land is intended for building, or a building is in the course of erection, or there is a building unconnected to a sewer, enquiries should be made of both the local authority and the regional water authority if the land abuts onto a highway, regarding any proposal for payment of costs of sewering to be borne by frontagers. A local land charge is not registrable until the building is erected and notice for payment served.

Water rights: Where water rights are of particular importance, eg purchase of riparian land, need to abstract inland water, or discharge of trade effluent into a stream, detailed research is recommended, directed to the Land Drainage Act 1961, as amended.

Listed Buildings: If the building is likely to be of architectural or historic interest then the relevant Part II enquiries should be raised with the local authority as to whether it is listed, whether a preservation or repairs notice has been served, whether there has been any application for listed building consent or whether a listed building enforcement notice has been served. The purchaser should be warned of all the restrictions and obligations involved if the building is listed or appears likely to be listed.

Planning permission and building regulations: Copies of planning consents and building regulation permits should be inspected to ascertain that all conditions have been complied with.

National House-Building Council: If the house was built within the last ten years a building society will ask for an NHBC Agreement and Notice of Insurance Cover. Check that these have been supplied by the vendor.

Damp-proofing and infestation treatment etc: Where there have been specialised works to a building it is necessary to inspect the estimates and guarantees to ascertain exactly what areas of the building are protected and to require that the guarantees be assigned to the purchaser.

Electricity supply: It may be necessary to check with the electricity board that the premises have a standard supply in order to avoid risk of expense to the purchaser arising on change of ownership.

Coal mining areas: Where minerals are extracted from beneath the ground there is the possibility of land subsidence. The National Coal Board have certain rights to withdraw the natural support from the surface and it is important to know as early as possible before contract whether the property is, or is likely to be, affected. Compensation is payable for damage resulting to buildings but if a building was erected after public notice had been given of the Board's intention to withdraw support, compensation is severely limited. In an area subject to subsidence a search should be made under the Coal Industry Nationalisation Act 1946, to discover whether a notice has been issued and whether there are proposals for future workings. Application is made to the Area Surveyor and Minerals Manager of the National Coal Board at the appropriate office. An official search is issued at a fixed fee with an extra charge for any further technical information required. The search will reveal past workings and any subsidence caused, proposed future workings with an estimate of subsidence, and the proximity of opencast workings. The Opencast Coal Act 1958 s.4 as amended, provides for compulsory rights orders granting temporary rights to the National Coal Board of use and occupation of land. Such orders are registrable as local land charges.

Companies: If the vendor is a company a search should be made in the Companies Register. Before 1970 a fixed charge to secure money on land owned by a company could be registered either in the Companies Register or in the land charges register; a post-1969 charge must be registered in the land charges register to bind a purchaser of unregistered land; to bind a creditor, including a mortgagee, it must be registered in the Companies Register. A floating charge whenever created is protected if registered in either or both the land charges register and the Companies Register. Where the title to the land is registered a purchaser will not be affected by a charge unless it is registered in the Land Registry. However, a search in the Companies Register will be a check against irregularities, eg a company may have changed its name and failed to notify the Land Registry, or the name may have been struck off the Companies Register. A transfer in such event could be void and the Land Registry could rectify against the purchaser. It appears that winding-up searches should be made in the Companies Register for voluntary liquidation and in the Companies Court for compulsory liquidation. Ideally both searches should be repeated shortly before completion. There is no provision for an official search and the search gives no protection or priority to the purchaser. Normally arrangement is made with an agent for a personal search and the result reported by letter for a fee.

Matrimonial Homes Act 1967: If the sale is by a sole vendor it may be wise to enquire whether he/she is married and, if so, make a search for a Class F Land Charge or, if the title is registered, for a notice or caution in the Land Register; see Matrimonial Homes Act 1967 as amended. The search will not prevent registration of such an interest between contract and completion.

8. Replies to enquiries

Replies to enquiries and entries revealed by the various searches should be carefully checked keeping in mind the purchaser's requirements. If any doubt remains further enquiry should be made. The client should be warned against exchange of contracts until replies to up-to-date searches have been received.

A contract made "subject to satisfactory searches" is a potential source of litigation. However, The Law Society's Conditions (1984) provides protection in this situation if it cannot be avoided. Negligence claims rarely arise in consequence of omission by the purchaser's solicitor to make local authority enquiries and searches, but result from failure to follow up the potential consequences of matters revealed in the local authority's replies and failure to warn the client of possible liabilities under such matters as any general financial charges registered, or the effects of slum clearance programmes, general improvement areas, road improvements, and town planning schemes. Information obtained informally from an official of a local planning authority, even in writing, may not be safely relied upon. One would have to be certain that the official had delegated power personally to make decisions and that a statement, eg as to the authorised use of the land, or that new plannng permission was unnecessary, constituted a determination within the legislation and binding on the authority.

9. Mortgage arrangements

Check that a mortgage offer in acceptable terms will be made before contracts are exchanged, that any conditions can be fulfilled and the advance will be available by the proposed completion date. If the mortgagee intends to retain part of the advance until some condition is fulfilled, eg specified work is to be carried out on the property, an alternative source must be found to cover the amount retained until the condition can be met. Where an offer from a building society is not sufficient in total, check whether a better offer can be obtained elsewhere. If the client is a woman, or the purchase is by a married couple, ascertain that the woman's earnings have been fully taken into account; see Sex Discrimination Act 1975. Check whether the advance could be improved by a top-up life assurance policy.
If instructed to act for the purchaser's building society, acknowledge instructions (Appendix 2, Letter P6).

10. Client's concurrent sale and purchase

This is an appropriate time to check the progress of any concurrent sale to ensure that both the sale and purchase are kept in line and to ascertain the reason if one side is being delayed.

11. Approval of the draft contract

When the terms of the contract have been agreed between the

solicitors make a full report to the client on replies received to preliminary enquiries, on searches, on enquiries of authorities, and on any observations arising from inspection of the property (Appendix 2, letter P7). Ensure that he understands exactly what is, and is not, included in the contract and is aware of all the obligations and limitations contained therein and their effect. Explain that on exchange he will become the owner in equity but the vendor will have the right to remain in possession as legal owner until completion. If the purchase is by two or more persons jointly ensure that they understand the legal effect of joint purchase and the possibility and effect of subsequent severance of a joint tenancy.

If dealing with an assignment of an existing lease the purchasing client should be supplied with a copy of the lease and the terms and covenants must be fully explained.

Ensure that the agreed completion date gives ample time for the purchaser to be in a position to complete lest a claim for interest or damages be incurred on default; see *Raineri* v *Miles* (1980).

Check that there is an agreed list of chattels being sold separately and that there is no doubt as to which chattels, fittings, etc are or are not included in the sale price of the property.

Check that the contract complies in all details with the requirements of the Law of Property Act 1925 s.40.

Check that both copies of the contract are identical. Subsequent additions or alterations have been held not to be within the solicitor's ostensible or implied authority.

The top copy of the draft contract can be returned to the vendor's solicitor, "approved as drawn" or "approved as amended". The covering letter should state that the matter is still "subject to contract" (Appendix 2, Letter P5).

12. Exchange of contracts

Exchange must not take place until all financial arrangements have been made and any necessary mortgage offer has been received. Check that all conditions in the mortgage offer can be complied with.

When consents are necessary for the assignment of a lease it is unwise to exchange contracts until these have been obtained.

Confirm that the property will be covered by insurance from the moment of exchange (Appendix 2, Letter P9). It is wise to draw the purchasing client's attention to this important matter in writing.

Both parties must expressly authorise exchange of contracts after being made fully aware of the legal consequences. Obtain signatures to the contract of all parties to the purchase. (In due course check that the signatures of all parties to the sale are on the vendor's part of the contract or, if the sale is by a sole vendor who is married, that the spouse also signs the contract or provides an undertaking against subsequent registration under the Matrimonial Homes Act 1967 as amended.)

The vendor's solicitor will send his part of the contract, or an engrossment if there have been amendments, to his client for signature in preparation for exchange, with any necessary explanation of the terms (Appendix 2, Letter V8).

If the purchase depends on a concurrent sale, then the signed contract for the sale of the client's present property and the deposit should be in hand before parting with his purchase contract.

Generally no contract comes into existence without actual exchange of the vendor's and purchaser's parts of the contract although it may be held that by their conduct the parties have waived the necessity for formal exchange. As to when exchange actually occurs, The Law Society's Conditions provide it is on posting of the second part; the National Conditions ignore the point (Appendix 2, Letters P8, V9).

In a chain of transactions the situation is dangerous and made more so by the almost inevitable use of the telephone; see *Domb* v *Isoz* (1980), and The Law Society's suggested formulae for *Exchanging Contracts by Telephone or Telex* in Law Society's Gazette, Feb 1980, p.144. Exchange by telephone or telex is included in The Law Society's Conditions (1984), but the dangers of informal exchange should be borne in mind.

Write to the client confirming that contracts have been exchanged, as instructed (Appendix 2, Letters V10, P10).

The sale of freehold property and the assignment of an existing lease or underlease is continued at Chapter 6.

Chapter 4

The new lease or underlease

1. Checklist: lessor

- Check the ownership of the property, the equitable position, occupancy and interests of other parties.
- Check any mortgage on the property for restrictions on the power of leasing. Commercial mortgages may impose severe restrictions, eg a public house may be tied to a brewery, or a filling station to an oil company. Prior consent of the mortgagee is usually required depending on the mortgage terms.
- With the grant of an underlease, check the head lease and any intermediate lease for restrictions on subletting or parting with possession, any required consents, and any provisions for earlier determination. The head lessor may require to see the terms of the underlease before giving consent, and it may be wise to omit the proposed rent from the draft. While he is entitled to check the legal provisions of an underlease, he is not entitled to know the rent unless the head lease contains a provision to that effect. All consents must be signed by the person giving the consent, not by his solicitor or agent.
- Check the title for easements or other rights, restrictive covenants or other obligations, which need to be incorporated in the leasehold terms.
- Ensure that the use for which the lease is being granted has planning permission or is an existing use and is in conformity with any restrictions on superior leases and the freehold reversion; if not the lease may be rescinded for misrepresentation.
- Investigate the position between the lessor and anyone having superior title for disputes or pending claims.
- Visit the property. Pay particular attention to access and boundaries. If necessary take measurements and check that

plans held are adequate. Where the demise is to be part of a building such as a residential flat or a suite of offices, inspect the common parts. If there are to be leases of parts of a building, surveyor's detailed plans will be necessary.

● Ascertain the present state of repair and advise on a survey; supply the surveyor with a copy of the draft lease or underlease when prepared.

Seek any necessary consents without delay.

2. References

Once the required consents have been received investigate the credentials of the proposed grantee carefully. It is important particularly with a business lease for the lessor to have a reliable tenant who will not default on the covenants in the lease. It may be wise to obtain a bank reference, a personal reference, and a business reference. If appropriate make a search of the Companies Register. If the company grantee does not appear to be substantial consider whether there ought to be a guarantor.

3. Draft contract

Although it is possible for the lease to come into existence on exchange of lease and counterpart lease without a prior contract, consider whether in the circumstances there should be a particularly carefully worded formal contract, subject to the usual terms of exchange. It is wise to have a contract where a substantial premium is being paid, where newly erected property is to be leased, or where there is to be a long domestic leasehold.

If there is to be a contract it is advisable to use the latest edition of a recognised standard form such as The Law Society's Contract for Sale, or the National Conditions of Sale. The contract for the grant of a lease or underlease will be in similar form to that for a sale or assignment, as considered in Chapter 2. If a considerable premium is to be paid, a deposit will be required as on the sale of freehold.

The draft lease or underlease must be prepared before the terms of the contract can be settled. The draft should be attached to the contract and referred to therein to avoid later dispute as to the terms agreed or as to what constitutes "usual", or "common", or "trade" covenants.

Compliance with the Law of Property Act 1925 s.40 requires particular attention with leasehold property as every clause must be evidenced in writing. In *Harvey* v *Pratt* (1965), the Court of Appeal affirmed that the absence of the date on which the lease was to commence rendered the contract unenforceable.

It is wise to head all correspondence "subject to contract", or if there is not to be a contract, "subject to lease".

4. Draft lease or underlease

The contents of the lease will vary according to the type of property, whether residential or business, length of term, rent provisions etc. The draft should meet the requirements of the lessor for this particular transaction. To ensure that no point is overlooked it is advisable to work through a suitable precedent, checking each clause carefully. The following points should be borne in mind:

(a) Parties

Check spellings carefully. Ensure that the lessor's/landlord's name is as it appears on his conveyance, or headlease if subletting.

(b) Recitals

Where there is a preliminary contract to grant a lease or underlease, this should be recited. Terms in the contract may be held to be collateral and not to have merged in the lease or underlease. In dealing with a block of flats it should be made apparent from a recital that there is a scheme covering all the flats to make it clear that the burden of the restrictions on each tenant is annexed to the demised flat, and the benefit to all the other flats.

(c) Consideration and receipt clause

This will be as for freehold, mentioning the premium (if any) but include as part of the consideration the rent and covenants on the part of the tenant "hereinafter reserved". The usual form will include the words, "in consideration of the sum of £... paid by the tenant to the landlord on or before execution hereof (the receipt whereof the landlord hereby acknowledges) and of the rent and covenants on the part of the tenant and conditions hereinafter reserved and contained".

(d) Definitions clause

If the lease is lengthy, or there is to be a standard lease for a number of units in a building, a definitions clause may usefully avoid repetition and uncertainty. In drafting a standard lease for flats care must be taken to adapt the definitions to relate to each particular flat. The definitions can be confined to describing the landlord, tenant, and the demised premises, but may include any item required. Where the demised premises are defined in this clause it is usually by reference to a schedule which contains the parcels.

In a complex lease it may be wise also to include an interpretation clause. With an underlease, any definitions and interpretation clauses will need to include reference to the superior lease and superior lessor.

(e) Parcels

The parcels clause must contain a detailed and accurate description of the property that is to pass to the tenant and must not contain more or less than is intended, either expressly or by implication. All that is included in the demise must be defined. It is essential to define which parts of the boundary walls and floors, and whether ceilings and windows, are included. Modern methods of building construction make it important to refer to particular layers in the horizontal boundaries. It should be made clear whether a ground floor flat includes the foundations, or the top flat includes the roof and structure thereon, depending on whether or not the liability for structural repairs and maintenance is to be imposed on the landlord or tenant. If it appears that the roof is included in the demise, the landlord may have difficulty in preventing the tenant from subsequently adding a further storey.

Where a building is divided into several flats or separate parts, the property should be described by reference to an accurate plan of adequate scale, preferably with the dimensions marked. A plan showing the curtilage is necessary if there are to be ancillary rights such as parking space, or an area for placing dustbins. This should be prepared by a surveyor or based on the Ordnance Survey map which has been competently checked with the land. Fences appurtenant to the property should be identified with T-marks, and party walls with H-marks, and if there is a separate garage it must be clearly indicated. With a business lease such a plan will be of particular importance as the dimensions are likely to have a bearing on the commercial value.

The plan should be able to be construed as part of the deed. If the accuracy of the plan cannot be relied on, it is unwise to include in the deed expressions such as, "the accuracy of the plan is not guaranteed" or, "for identification purposes" but rather it should be stated that, "the plan does not limit or enlarge the description in the parcels".

All necessary rights should be specifically set out. It is unwise to rely on the rights implied by the Law of Property Act 1925 s.62. The section will not imply the grant of services often provided by a landlord, such as hot water and heating; neither will rights of access imply parking facilities.

Rights of way, parking rights, and turning areas with access to and from the highway and the building, should be clearly shown on the plan which defines any garage or car-port. Consider whether a clause is needed to restrict parking which may cause obstruction. Right of access and rights over and under adjoining property in connection with the supply and maintenance of drainage, water, gas, electricity, and other services, should be expressly stated and clearly shown on the plan. Similarly, where the lease is of part of a building, rights of support should be set out as should rights over common parts of the building.

It is wise to insert a clause preventing the tenant from acquiring any rights, privileges or easements in respect of the demised premises or adjoining land other than those expressly given by the lease. Be careful not to grant rights which subsequently could be enlarged; see *V T Engineering Ltd* v *Richard Barland & Co Ltd* (1968).

If a proposed right coincides with a right of another tenant or with the landlord's reservation, ensure that they are stated in precisely the same terms.

(f) Exceptions and reservations

An exceptions clause will be required if the landlord wishes to retain an existing right in the property. A reservation refers to a newly created right.

The landlord must specifically reserve all necessary rights of support, way, water, drainage, access, etc as no such rights will be implied. Where appropriate the right should contain the words "in common with (the grantor) and all others having a like right", or similar wording. Ensure he reserves any rights required for present and future use and enjoyment of adjoining and neighbouring property he owns; if he might wish to develop adjoining land he must reserve rights of light and air.

He must secure the right to enter the demised premises to inspect the state of repair or to check the fixtures and fittings. He must also reserve sufficient rights to enable him to ascertain that the tenant is complying with his covenants.

In a business lease it may be necessary to reserve, for example, a right to exhibit advertisements on external walls of a building or on a forecourt used for parking.

(g) Habendum

The habendum will state the date of commencement and the duration of the term. The date should be precisely defined as anniversaries may be important for service of notices under the lease, particularly with regard to rent reviews. To avoid uncertainty, the term should be stated to commence "on" a certain date, not "from" that date, and it can be stated to commence on a past, present, or future date.

In drafting an underlease the term should be at least one day less than the term of the head or superior lease to preserve the grantor's reversionary interest.

In granting a business underlease consider the advisability of restricting the term to expire not less than fourteen months before the date of expiry of the head lease, so that the underlessor will qualify as the "competent landlord" under the Landlord and Tenant Act 1954 s.44.

(h) Reddendum

The amount of rent must be fixed, and the dates on which it is to be paid precisely stated, although future rent may be affected by a rent review clause. Rent should be made payable in advance and due whether or not demand is made.

If the term of the lease is stated to run from a date earlier than completion of the grant, it must be made clear that the rent is payable from the date of the lease, not commencement of the term. If rent is to be payable on the next quarter day there should be provision for an apportionment.

With an underlease, consider the date on which the head rent falls due. It will be to the lessor's advantage to receive the rent on the underlease before he has to pay his own rent; where the head rent is due on the usual quarter days, ie 25 March, 24 June, 29 September, and 25 December, consider whether rent on the underlease should be required on the first day of each of those months.

Payment for services, repairs, and other outgoings are usually in arrear, but should be expressed as additional rent to facilitate recovery of such monies due. Ensure that these are not affected by rent review provisions.

It is reasonable to provide cesser or suspension of rent if the premises become so seriously damaged as to be uninhabitable, but the landlord may wish for a proviso for determination of the term by service of notice if for any reason reinstatement is impracticable. This is safer than relying on the doctrine of frustration, although this doctrine can apply to a lease. See *National Carriers Ltd* v *Panalpina (Northern) Ltd* (1981).

(i) Rent review clause

Residential lease: Any rent review clause should provide for fixed increases at fixed periods; terms for fixing a "market rent" or a rent "to be agreed between the parties", are unsuitable for residential property. Ensure that a rent review will not bring the property within the scope of the Rent Acts. See Rent Act 1977 as amended by Housing Act 1980 s.78 and H. C. Adamson; Law Society's Gazette, Oct 1980 p.1069. If the rent is raised to greater than two-thirds of the rateable value there is a possibility of creating a protected tenancy.

If the head lease contains a rent review clause there will need to be earlier, or perhaps more frequent, rent reviews in the underlease.

The lease should provide that in serving of any notice by the landlord time should not be of the essence.

Business lease: Rent review clauses are commonly inserted and provide the period for review and the machinery for fixing the amount of the revised rent.

Consider the following:

- *Periodic revision to market rent* — The review clause must provide the date for service of notice by the landlord, and the procedure for fixing the amount of the revised rent. It should state that time is not to be of the essence in respect of such service. The clause may provide that the tenant must serve a counter notice if he objects to the landlord's proposals. In the event of the parties failing to reach agreement within a specified period the matter should be settled by arbitration; see *Thomas Bates & Son Ltd* v *Wyndham's (Lingerie) Ltd* (1981) and *Beer* v *Bowden* (1981). In the interim period the present rent will be received as payment on account of the revised rent when fixed. It would be prudent to specify a rate of interest to be paid on any amount outstanding.
- *Index-linked rent* — The rent may be linked to movements in a suitable price index, eg the Index of Retail Prices pub-

lished by the Department of Employment. While this avoids the necessity for arbitration, the client should be advised of the disadvantages such as constant fluctuation and the fact that the rent need not reflect the true market value of the property.

Where there is a rent review clause in the head lease, this will affect the date and term to be drafted for rent reviews in an underlease.

In a long lease consider whether there should be provision for review of the rent review clause, as price inflation may require more frequent rent reviews, or the machinery for determining the revised rent may become out-of-date.

A rent review clause needs to be drawn with great care and the client should be fully advised of its implications.

(j) Lessee's/tenant's covenants

These will vary according to the type of property and the length of term. It should be made clear which covenants are with the lessee alone and which are also with other lessees.

- *To pay reserved rent as provided without deductions.*

- *To pay all rates, taxes, assessments, impositions and outgoings levied or charged:* This will include all outgoings except any of a novel nature imposed by Parliament; in such case Parliament is likely to provide where the burden shall fall. The purpose of the covenant is to impose liability on the tenant and to indemnify the landlord for any payments he may have to make, so that reimbursement can be claimed as of right under the lease. The clause may include a provision for the landlord's surveyor to determine the proportion of any outgoings payable by the tenant but the surveyor's decision should not be made conclusive on matters of law as it may be held to be an attempt to oust the jurisdiction of the Court and void as contrary to public policy; in which case the clause may not be severable and much of the lease may be made void; see *Re Davstone Estate's Leases* (1969).

- *To pay certain other costs:* These will include the landlord's costs and expenses arising from recovery of rent and service of notices or proceedings under the Law of Property Act 1925 ss.146, 147. There may also be a covenant to pay legal costs and surveyor's fees arising from any application by the lessee for a licence or consent of the landlord as required by the lease, whether granted or refused or the application withdrawn.

● *To pay maintenance and service charges:* For both landlord and tenant this may prove to be the most troublesome and costly area in the lease and hence must be the most carefully drafted, taking into account current legislation and the considerable case law. If the landlord's services are more extensive than cleaning and lighting the common parts of the building, it may be convenient to set them out in a schedule and incorporate this by reference. In the case of flats, a suite of offices, a building divided into parts, or leasehold houses on an estate, there will be a comprehensively drawn covenant to contribute to the cost of upkeep of areas and things used in common with others entitled.

If the landlord is to be responsible for external repairs and maintenance, and to provide services at the tenant's expense, the covenant should expressly provide for the landlord to be able to build up a maintenance fund to meet future expenditure. This is permissible for flats under the Housing Act 1980, which allows payments to be made in advance of expenditure. The Act places within "service charges", services, repairs, maintenance, insurance, and management costs. Preliminary procedure is set out in Schedule 19 and, if not followed, the landlord may be unable to recover costs incurred on major works.

As to payment of service charges, if the amount is to be certified by the landlord's agent, surveyor, or accountant, it should be stated that the certificate shall be conclusive on matters of fact, not law, to avoid the problem shown in *Re Davstone.* However such a clause can be challenged if the landlord and agent are one and the same company; see *Finchbourne* v *Rodrigues* (1976).

It may be wise to provide for payment of interest on money which the landlord may need to borrow to finance works. It is certainly wise to provide for interest to be payable on service charges unpaid by the tenant one month from delivery of the demand.

The landlord must decide who is to manage the property and control expenditure of the maintenance fund, whether there are to be managing agents, or a management company in which every leaseholder will be required to hold a share; a management company is often the most convenient arrangement for buildings let in parts. There should then be a separate covenant in the lease to cover all matters relating to the management company. It is essential that there is no possibility of lapse of shareholding; there must be a strict obligation that shares are taken up on assignment of the lease. There should be provision for matters of title to shares, eg where a share is not registered in an assignee's name, he having died and his executor having failed to deal with the shareholding.

● *To repair:* Ensure that the tenant's obligations are not inconsistent with other covenants requiring contribution to maintenance carried out by the landlord, payment of outgoings, and compliance with statutory requirements of local and other authorities.

The type of structure and type of premises, whether it be flat, house, factory building, shop unit or suite of offices will largely determine the division of responsibility for repair between landlord and tenant. No area of the property must escape the responsibility to repair.

The extent of the tenant's liability for repair should be consistent with the length of the leasehold term and the age of the building. In a short lease the covenant to repair may be restricted to internal or decorative repair and to keeping fixtures and fittings in repair; extensive repairs ought not to be required, nor should the tenant be expected to do works to improve an old building.

On the grant of an underlease ensure that the liability for repairs by the underlessee is sufficient to satisfy the terms of the headlease and require from the underlessee a covenant of indemnity.

To except the tenant from structural repairs may relieve him from repairs to windows, doors, floors, skirtings, plasterwork, and glass and wood partitioning.

If the tenant is to be liable for internal repairs then the lease should define whether windows and the outside of access doors and door furniture are included.

The period for internal decoration is usually in every seventh year. It is wise to provide also for redecoration in the last year of the tenancy, howsoever terminated.

As the demise includes the fixtures it is unnecessary to mention repair or renewal of any of them specifically unless a special provision is required for a particular item and it should then be made clear that the rest of the fixtures are not thereby excluded from the general requirement to repair or replace.

In a business lease, most of the fittings will probably be

"trade fixtures" which will remain the property of the tenant; there may, however, be landlord's fixtures such as a central heating system which must be kept in repair.

Where obligations for external repairs and decorations are to be imposed, the type of structure and materials used in the building must be appropriately provided for. Be wary of old precedents which may refer to timber when the structure is of steel and concrete, or to redecoration by graining and varnishing when the surfaces are unlikely to be suitable for such treatment, or to "good oil paint" which is now largely superseded. A covenant to paint should define the manner in which the work is to be done, including the number of coats and type of paint.

Where the property is one of several adjoining houses as in a terrace, it is probably necessary to require uniformity of external painting or other treatment. This may be achieved by providing that the landlord shall carry out the work at the tenant's expense. In this case the lease should provide that the landlord has a right to repair any defective parts, such as gutters, before painting. Such a clause will avoid the landlord having to stop the work to obtain the tenant's consent.

Where there are external repairing covenants for buildings let in parts a management company in which all tenants are shareholders is generally the most convenient device.

Where there are houses on an estate there will be obligations in respect of maintenance of fences, pipes, wires and cables, and perhaps party walls. Obligation to repair party walls should include liability for a deficiency of support, and it will be necessary to include rights of access to adjoining property. (It may be necessary to have similar provision with a flat for party floors.)

Obligations to maintain a section of a right of way can be placed on the tenant so long as default powers are reserved to the landlord.

An obligation to keep the demised property adequately fenced will ensure that if a fence becomes past repair the tenant must replace it.

● *To yield up in repair:* Repairing covenants may be followed by a covenant to yield up the premises at the expiry or determination of the lease, however determined, in a proper state of repair.

- *To permit the landlord to enter and view the state of repair:*
  This is essential and provision should be made for serving
  notice of lack of repair, and a right for the landlord to enter
  and carry out works not done, the costs and expenses
  incurred to be a debt recoverable by action. During the final
  years of a long term there should be a right to enter and take
  an inventory of fixtures and fittings. If necessary a
  covenant should be included to permit the landlord and all
  persons authorised by him to enter to carry out alterations
  and repairs to any adjoining premises owned by him.

- *To insure:* The insurance clause requires clear instructions
  from the client and careful drafting. Besides fire, other
  risks should be covered such as damage by storm, tempest,
  flood, damage from aircraft, impact damage by vehicles,
  and riots and vandalism.

  In a long lease the cost of insurance is usually placed on the
  tenant. The landlord should require the insurance to be in
  the joint names of the landlord and tenant and there should
  be provision for endorsement on the policy of other parties'
  interests, as both the landlord and the tenant may have
  mortgagees who require their interests to be noted. The
  insurance should be with an insurance office approved by
  the landlord and the amount of the cover should be
  sufficient for reinstatement of the building; there will,
  therefore, be need to provide for increased cover to meet
  increasing building costs. The client may need advice from
  his surveyor on the quantum of such costs and problems
  involved if the building is an old one which could not
  reasonably be rebuilt similarly if totally destroyed by fire.
  The tenant should be required to produce on demand the
  receipt for the last premium paid. A covenant to insure with
  a named company binds the tenant to take out the
  company's usual policy even though it excludes some
  specific risk. The tenant will not be liable if the property is
  destroyed in a way excepted from the policy; see *Upjohn* v
  Hitchens (1918). Where there is a covenant to insure in the
  joint names of landlord and tenant and to expend the policy
  monies on reinstatement, should it be impossible to
  reinstate, the tenant will be entitled to retain the money, as
  the insurance is to provide security only for the tenant's,
  not the landlord's, liability to reinstate; see *Re King* (1963).

  The landlord may wish to insure at the tenant's expense
  rather than have to check that the tenant does not allow the
  policy to lapse. He is under no obligation to insure as

cheaply as possible, and the tenant cannot insist on some alternative policy, but he should be supplied with a copy of the policy and be notified of any subsequent alteration. The insurance requirements should not be such that they would be unacceptable to a mortgagee.

Where the demised premises are part of a building, the landlord should insure the whole property and require the tenant to contribute to the cost, usually by apportionment under the general maintenance payments. The insurance cover should extend to shared facilities such as lifts, boilers, and other equipment.

Where the landlord covenants to insure at the tenant's expense, he is likely to be liable to reinstate a building destroyed even in the absence of a covenant to do so, for such a covenant has been held to benefit both landlord and tenant; see *Mumford Hotels Ltd* v *Wheeler* (1964). The landlord may not want to be committed to reinstate, either because the insurance monies may prove to be insufficient or because the building is an old one. There may be delays which hamper rebuilding and he may wish a clause to be inserted to absolve him from liability for such delays.

● *User:* The restrictions will largely depend upon the type of property. In a residential lease there should be an absolute covenant to use as a private dwelling. A covenant against immoral user gives the landlord a straightforward remedy for breach.

With business premises restrictions on use will seriously affect the market value, although the landlord's own business activity within the same area must be considered. There should be a proviso for consent to change of use. The landlord must not demand payment as a condition of giving his consent but he may claim for loss of value of the premises and for legal and other expenses incurred. There should be a requirement for the tenant to comply with Town and Country Planning legislation and not to apply for planning permission without the landlord's written consent.

The use must comply with any restrictive covenants on superior leases or the freehold reversion.

● *To deliver and comply with notices:* The tenant should be required to provide the landlord with a copy of any notice or order served by an authority on the tenant or any sub-tenant within seven days of receipt. There should be an obligation to comply with such notice or order at his own expense, or to join with the landlord if so requested in raising objections or appealing.

- *Not to assign or sublet:* It is usual with a short-term tenancy to prohibit assignment and sub-letting but otherwise absolute prohibitions are best avoided as they may render the property less marketable and less attractive to a mortgagee. A prohibition restricting assignment without the landlord's consent during the last seven years of a long lease would not be unreasonable, and it is usual to provide for an absolute prohibition against assignment, sub-letting, or parting with possession, of part only of the property.

  Where a commercial lease includes living accommodation, eg shop premises with a flat above, it should be expressly provided that the living accommodation must not be separately sub-let to avoid the risk of creating a "protected tenancy".

  If consent is to be required then it will be implied that such consent must not be unreasonably withheld, but provision can be made that the landlord shall not be required to consent to any assignment or sub-letting which may diminish his security. This will include assignment to a limited company or any action which would bring the property within the ambit of the Rent Acts. If the landlord requires that the tenant shall first offer to surrender the lease this will require registration as an estate contract to bind successors in title; see *Greene* v *Church Commissioners for England* (1974), also *Allnatt London Properties Ltd* v *Newton* (1981).

  It has been held unreasonable unless the lease so provides, for a landlord to require personal guarantees from the directors of a limited company to which assignment is proposed, and it is wise to include such provision. However, difficulties associated with assignments to limited companies may be avoided by inserting a covenant requiring personal residence; such a lease is not assignable to a limited company; see *Jenkins* v *Price* (1908).

  The Law of Property Act 1925 s.48(1), makes void any stipulation in a lease or underlease that assignments of the lessee's or underlessee's interests shall be prepared by the lessor's solicitor at the purchaser's expense.

- *To register assignments or sub-letting:* There should be a stipulation requiring the tenant to register any assignment, sub-letting, devolution, or mortgage, with the landlord's solicitor within a specified but reasonable period on payment of a prescribed fee plus VAT. A landlord is not entitled to make a profit for himself out of a proposed assignment but he can secure himself against loss. Breach of the stipulation will enable the landlord to enforce the conditions for re-entry in the lease.

● *Not to make alterations or improvements:* It is wise to insert an express covenant requiring the landlord's consent to any alterations or improvements to the property. As this is a qualified covenant statute will imply that consent to improvements must not be unreasonably withheld. Whether the covenant is absolute or qualified the tenant of a business premises may apply to the Court for authority to carry out improvements.

● *Restrictions:* A covenant against causing nuisance or annoyance to owners, tenants, or occupiers of neighbouring premises is important as providing a remedy which will maintain the amenity value of the premises, and may provide an extra remedy in case of breach of other covenants. In a block of flats there may need to be a covenant against noise with express provision against music between certain hours of the night, and a requirement for provision of floor coverings to deaden sound. There should be a restriction against keeping birds or animals without consent, and consider whether restrictions are required on the parking of cars, placing of dustbins, hanging-out washing, bonfires, the erection of outdoor aerials, and the display of advertising signs etc.

● *To observe all covenants and restrictions:* There should be a covenant by the tenant to observe all the restrictions set out in the lease and, so far as applicable, the tenant's covenants and obligations in any head lease. The terms of an underlease must not be inconsistent with the terms of the head lease but subject to this proviso, the underlease need not follow the wording of the head lease and may contain different provisions, eg earlier rent review dates.

It may be convenient to supply a copy of the covenants in the head lease, omitting the head rent, and to recite that the tenant having been supplied with such copy accepts and covenants to perform, and to indemnify the grantor against proceedings by the head lessor.

● *Provision limiting statutory compensation:* This will provide that the tenant under a business lease shall not be entitled to compensation under the provisions of the

Landlord and Tenant Act 1954 s.37 on quitting unless the conditions in s.38(2) of the Act are satisfied. This clause should be inserted in any business lease where the lease is for a term exceeding five years.

● *An independent right of entry:* This can be imposed in order to remedy any breach of covenant and imposes a right to recover the cost of work required to be executed, as a debt.

(k) Lessor's/landlord's covenants

When drafting the covenants which the landlord will be required to give, keep in mind the tenant's covenants as the two must not be inconsistent; also keep in mind the type of property and what will be expedient and reasonable in this particular case.

● *Quiet enjoyment:* The tenant has a right to quiet enjoyment and this may be the only covenant by the landlord, but in the absence of an express covenant it will be implied. It is usually stated that "the tenant shall and may peaceably hold the demised premises during the term without any lawful interruption by the landlord or any person rightfully claiming under or in trust for the landlord". This will not protect an underlessee against the acts of a superior lessor or the freeholder.

● *To insure:* This is as discussed in *lessee's covenants*, see page 49.

● *To repair:* Ensure that the landlord's and tenant's specific repairing covenants together cover all the works of repair likely to arise, not only to the structure, roof and foundations, but also to the common parts, eg entrance and stairs.

A landlord's covenant to keep the structure in repair should identify what comprises the structure of the particular building and, in a modern building, should include responsibility for reinstatement even though the defects which have arisen are the result of faulty design, negligent building methods, or defective materials. It was held in *Smedley* v *Chumley and Hawke Ltd* (1981) that a landlord's covenant to keep the main walls and roof in good structural repair required them to be kept in repair, even when defective foundations made damage inevitable.

In certain leases of residential property the landlord may be under a statutory obligation to repair, in which case the parties cannot contract out; see Housing Act 1961.

● *To provide services:* In the absence of an express provision the Courts are reluctant to imply a contractual obligation to provide services. These may be confined to cleaning and lighting the common parts of the building or extend to the provision of hot water and central heating, lifts, porterage, and removal of refuse. The provision of hot water can be restricted to reasonable hours, and heating to reasonable hours and periods of the year, all of which should be specified. It is unwise to specify a temperature to be maintained; it is preferable to state "adequate heating". Provision of lift services requires careful drafting and must protect the landlord against liability arising from breakdown or vandalism; liability for injury must be covered by insurance. It is unwise to provide for a resident porter as it may be found that the building can be efficiently run by a non-resident person. Liability for suspension of porterage should be excluded.

Provision of services to business premises should be qualified, eg heating restricted to specified periods, lift services confined to opening hours of the building. However, the minimum standard of the services must be sufficient to meet the tenant's obligation to staff under the Offices, Shops and Railway Premises Act 1963, but the landlord should be relieved of liability for any breakdown, deficiency or unavoidable suspension of services.

Services should be restricted to those parts of the premises to which the tenant has access. A clause should be inserted to protect the landlord against liability for the negligence of any person or company employed to perform the services, and against any strike or other industrial dispute.

When drafting this clause keep in mind the tenant's covenants to pay service charges. If services are extensive it may be convenient to list them in a schedule and incorporate this by reference.

● *To appoint an arbitrator under any arbitration provision in the lease:* This may be required by the tenant of a unit or flat to determine any dispute between the tenant and any other tenant concerning matters in the lease.

(l) Arbitration

It should be considered whether an arbitration clause is likely to be advantageous as a means of settling disputes between landlord and tenant. Such a clause should be in comprehensive terms and without ambiguity.

In a block of flats the landlord may covenant, if required by the tenant, to appoint an arbitrator under any arbitration provision to determine disputes between the various tenants concerning matters in the lease.

Most precedents suggest that the arbitrator should be appointed either by the President of The Law Society or by the President of the Royal Institution of Chartered Surveyors, but the choice need not be so restricted.

In a business lease so many of the disputes are likely to involve points of law, or fall within the provisions of the Landlord and Tenant Act 1954, that a Court hearing may be more appropriate than arbitration.

(m) Provisos

- *Re-entry:* This will provide for the landlord to re-enter and determine the lease for breach of covenant to pay rent within a prescribed period, and the words, "whether legally demanded or not" should be included to avoid procedural difficulty. This right will not be implied. There should be a similar right for breach of other covenants or conditions in the lease. Provision can be made for bankruptcy or the liquidation of the tenant or his guarantor to give rise to this right; however, if the tenant is paying a premium for the lease with the aid of a mortgage, the mortgagee may refuse an advance if the lease contains such a provision, so the proposed transaction may fail. The right of re-entry should be stated not to exclude other rights and remedies available to the landlord.

- *Purchase of reversion or renewal of the lease:* This option needs careful drafting, particularly as to the method for fixing the price for purchase of the reversion, or the length of term and rent of the new lease. Where there is an option to renew there is a danger of creating a perpetually renewable lease. Compare *Caerphilly Concrete Products Ltd* v *Owen* (1972) with *Marjorie Burnett Ltd* v *Barclay* (1980). Make it clear who is entitled to exercise the option; specify time limits and make this right subject to performance by the tenant of his obligations under the lease.

- *Exclusion of landlord's liability:* The landlord should seek to exclude as far as possible liability for loss or injury suffered by the tenant or anyone else on the demised premises.

- *Contracting out of the Landlord and Tenant Act 1954:* If the consent of the Court has been obtained allowing the parties to a business lease to contract out of the security of tenure provisions in Part II of the Act a statement of the court's authority must be included in or endorsed on the lease.

(n) Certificate of value

Insert a certificate of value appropriate to current legislation relating to stamp duty.

(o) Testatum

(p) Schedules

Matters which can be well set out in schedules rather than in the body of the deed include the parcels; easements, rights and privileges included in the demise; exceptions and reservations; restrictions and covenants; and services provided by lessor.

(q) Execution and attestation

The lease will be executed by the lessor and the counterpart lease by the lessee.

5. Checklist

Ensure that:

- Client has good title and there are no impediments to entering into the transactions;
- There are no disputes affecting the property;
- All necessary consents and references have been obtained;
- All names and addresses are complete and correctly spelled;
- The parcels clause gives a detailed and accurate description of the property and the plan is correct;
- No rights have been given by implication which were not intended;

- All rights needed over retained land or common parts have been excepted or reserved;
- Starting date, term, rent, and times of payment are stated precisely;
- Rent review clauses have been clearly drafted as they are a likely area for dispute later;
- Landlord's and tenant's covenants complement each other so that no aspect is overlooked;
- Time is not to be of the essence for service of notices by the landlord;
- Arbitration clause is precise and certain;
- The effect of legislation on the proposed term has been considered;
- List of fixtures and fittings, if any, has been checked by client;
- Contract and draft lease are in accordance with client's instructions and his interests have been fully protected.

After checking the draft contract and the draft lease prepare two copies of each to be sent to the lessee's solicitor for his approval (Appendix 2, Letter V5).

6. Replies to preliminary enquiries

Where a standard lease is being provided for flats in a block, houses on an estate, or for commercial lettings such as rows of shops or blocks of offices, replies to enquiries on a standard form should be sent to the lessee's solicitor with draft contract and draft lease. Send also all other relevant material such as planning permission and building byelaw consent.

First check these replies carefully with the client, and check also replies to individual enquiries received later from the proposed lessee's solicitor (Appendix 2, Letters V6, V7). Bear in mind the Misrepresentation Act 1967 as discussed in Chapter 2. Particularly relevant to a commercial transaction will be the special knowledge which may be imputed to the lessor, or the special relationship created by the transaction, see *Esso Petroleum Co Ltd* v *Mardon* (1976).

Chapter 5

The new lease or underlease: approval

1. The contract

If there is to be a contract the lessee's solicitor should check carefully to ensure that it is a sound contract and, as far as possible, meets the requirements of his client (Appendix 2, Letter P4). Consider the following points:

(a) Title

Ascertain that the lessor has good title and can validly grant the proposed term. The Law Society have stated that, "they feel sure that ... solicitors acting for lessors will not put obstacles in the way of lessees who, because of the length of term, the premium to be paid, the money to be expended by them or some other special reason, seek to satisfy themselves that the proposed lessor is in fact entitled to grant the lease"; see *Law Society's Gazette* 1958 page 151.

If the lease will be the subject of first registration of title, the lessee must investigate the reversionary title in order to obtain an absolute leasehold title. If the title to the reversion cannot be deduced, require an express warranty to the effect that the title is good and marketable and the proposed lease will not contravene any restrictions on the reversion.

If the lease is of registered land it will be subject to incumbrances on the Register of the lessor's title and to overriding interests. If the reversionary title is unregistered make an index map search at the district land registry for the area (Land Registry Form 96).

Ascertain whether there are any:

- restrictions on the freehold or leasehold reversion. The Law of Property Act 1925 s.44(5) provides that where the purchaser has no right to investigate a superior title he is not affected by notice of matters which such investigation would have revealed. There will be no such protection where the matter is registered as a land charge, nor where the lease is of registered land.

- restrictions on the power of leasing contained in any mortgage or charge on the reversionary interest.
- persons having rights of occupation or overriding interests who are not parties to the contract. If there is a sole proprietor ascertain the marital status for the purpose of the Matrimonial Homes Act 1967 as amended.

An underlessee has no right under an open contract to have the freehold or reversionary title deduced, but may make enquiries about the lease out of which the underlease is being granted and any assignment thereof. Check the terms in the superior lease particularly regarding restrictions on leasing, on use of the premises and on the necessity for consents.

(b) Deposit

If a deposit is required check that it is not more than 10 per cent of the premium, and is to be held by the lessor's solicitor as stakeholder; see Chapter 3.

(c) Special conditions

Check any special conditions inserted in the contract; see Chapter 3.

(d) Searches and enquiries

Make local authority and other searches and enquiries, being especially concerned as to permitted use under planning legislation and any road proposals which may affect the value of the property. Extend the enquiries to cover adjacent areas. Raise preliminary enquiries as appropriate; see Chapter 3.

With the grant of an underlease require a copy of the lease out of which the underlease is to be granted to be supplied, and the original to be available for inspection on completion. Check any restrictions on the superior lease and if it contains favourable covenants require the benefit to be transmitted to the underlease.

2. The lease or underlease

Check that the draft meets the particular requirements of the client, and corresponds with his instructions. Consider the following points:

(a) Parcels

Insist that an accurate plan, preferably drawn by a surveyor, is incorporated by specific reference in the parcels. Do not accept a plan "for identification purposes only" unless a satisfactory explanation is given. If it is a newly divided property, the plan should be of a scale not less than 1/500, and clearly show overhangs and party walls. If the lessor's title is registered the title number should be included in the parcels. If the lease is for part only of the land the Land Registry will require a plan accurately defining the area, and signed by all parties.

Examine in detail the extent of the premises. Where the lease is of part of a building, check whether horizontal divisions (floors, ceilings), external sides of walls, window frames and glass, external doors and door furniture, etc are included in the demise. In a ground floor flat check whether foundations are included, in a top floor flat whether the roof is included. If the client has specified he requires a flat on the top floor check that it will not be possible for a storey to be added at some time in the future. Check ownership of boundaries and fences, and if part of a building, that boundaries are precisely defined.

The lessee should not rely on the Law of Property Act 1925 s.62, to imply sufficient rights and easements. Check that there is specific grant of all required, including access in connection with the supply of gas, water, electricity, telephone, drainage. In a business lease there may be special requirements such as Telex, and provision of facilities for loading and unloading goods. Check access rights to all parts of the premises at all times including dustbin area, garden, and to and from the highway. Check rights for garaging, access to garage, turning space, and parking. Check mutual access rights with neighbouring property necessary for repairs. On an estate, check there is a grant of easement for drains, pipes, wires, cables, and right of way together with the necessary access over adjoining property.

(b) Exceptions and reservations

The lessor will reserve rights to benefit the remainder of the property and neighbouring land he owns. Check that these are not unreasonable nor excessive particularly with respect to exclusion of rights to light and air. He will insist on the right to enter and inspect the state of the demised premises and, if necessary, remedy any failure by the lessee to repair, etc. Such right of access should be expressly confined to reasonable hours on giving due notice except in an emergency. There should be a provision requiring the lessor to make good after exercising any right or carrying out works on the premises, and to indemnify the lessee against claims arising from such works.

(c) Habendum

Ensure that the dates for commencement and duration of the term are certain and without ambiguity. Check that the term is as agreed and is not shortened by being expressed to have commenced at an earlier date. If an earlier date is accepted, check that it is clearly expressed that the rent is payable only from the date of the tenant's possession. Ensure that the commencement date does not adversely affect the tenant with regard to the imminence of a rent review.

In a long business lease the tenant will require a break clause probably at five-yearly intervals. It would be wise to consider in what other circumstances, such as destruction of the property, there should be a right to determine. It is usual to require six months notice in writing and the landlord will wish to make time of the essence for service of the notice by tenant. Ensure that the date for giving notice is after a rent review date, so that the tenant can determine the lease if he does not wish to pay the reviewed rent.

(d) Reddendum

Check that the amount of rent, and the dates for payment are certain. Is the rent to be paid in advance or in arrear? If interest is to be payable on overdue rent and other charges, require that it does not accrue until the landlord has served notice.

- *Rent review:* If there is a rent review clause compare the review date with the date of commencement of lease. Make sure that the date of review comes before any break clause date. The lease will usually provide that time is of the essence for service of notice of determination, not for service of notice of a rent increase. If the tenant is required to serve a counter notice objecting to the new rent, seek to delete this provision entirely, or delete any provision making time of the essence for serving such notice.

   Check that a rent review will not bring a residential property within the scope of the Rent Acts as this will prevent the tenant obtaining the market value should he wish to assign. Where in a business lease, a reviewed rent is to be a "market rent agreed by the parties", make sure that any improvements to the property by the tenant are not included in the assessment of the value of the property. If the parties cannot agree the revised rent there must be provision for reference to an expert or an arbitrator after a specified period, "in the absence of agreement", in case the parties have not attempted to agree. If the landlord requires reference to an expert, there should be provision for both parties to make representations to the expert, and to terminate the expert's powers if he fails to exercise due skill and care. A rent review may provide that the new rent shall not be less than the original rent. This term could prove onerous if some unforeseen circumstance, such as a road development, affected the profitability of the business. If the landlord insists on such a term there should be provision to enable the tenant to determine the lease after an unsatisfactory review.

An index-linked rent is more likely to be found in a business lease and could be burdensome to a tenant whose profits are not rising as quickly as the level of price inflation.

● *Suspension of rent:* It is essential for the tenant to have the right to suspend payment of rent and any service charge if the premises are made uninhabitable or unusable. It may be difficult to claim the lease has been frustrated. Check the clause to ensure that it provides that rent will not be payable until the premises are reinstated and the tenant is able to resume occupation. It may be desirable for the tenant to have the right to determine the lease if the premises are not fit for occupation after a period of time.

3. Lessee's/tenant's covenants

All tenant's covenants should be expressed to be "reasonable" or be qualified in some way to avoid breach of covenant where performance becomes difficult or impossible.

(a) To pay maintenance and service charges

If there is a covenant which provides that the landlord will maintain parts of the property, and provide services at the tenant's expense consider carefully:

● Provide client's surveyor with a copy of the lease and instruct him to inspect the demise and the condition of the whole building if appropriate.

● Ensure that building maintenance provisions do not include altering or rebuilding the structure.

- The clause will usually provide for a certificate of costs to be issued by the landlord's surveyor or other agent "who shall be the final arbiter" of amounts payable. Ensure that there is a requirement that such agent should be professionally qualified, that demand for professional fees should be restricted to "reasonable fees properly incurred", that the sum certified should be "fair and reasonable", and the certificate should be conclusive as to fact only.

- Ascertain that services to be provided by the landlord are clearly defined and that any specified charges will be adequate to fund these services.

- With a divided building, ascertain how sums for maintenance are to be allocated for the demised premises in relation to the rest of the building.

- The covenant should be so worded as to cast a positive duty on the landlord to carry out work and provide services to a proper and reasonable standard.

- Warn client of the risk of possible escalation of service charges. Draw his attention to the rights of tenants who pay service charges as set out in the Housing Act 1980.

It may be to the tenant's advantage that there is a reserve or sinking fund to meet the expense of unexpected or costly maintenance work. If there is, check that:

- it is certain what items of expenditure will be covered by the fund;

- there is an obligation for the fund to be used for such expenditure, rather than the current charge be increased;

- the landlord should contribute in respect of any part of the building covered by the fund but unlet;

- the balance of the fund shall be placed in a special bank deposit account and interest credited to the fund;

- the existence of the fund will not prejudice any insurance claim if the building is destroyed;

- the landlord is required to disclose all information regarding the fund including the tenant's current balance.

With residential flats or divided property it is not unusual for a tenants' company to maintain the exterior and common parts of the property. If this applies check that:

- the company has power to levy charges sufficient to cover its liabilities;

- there is a suitable arrangement to regulate the accounts if some members fail to pay their contribution;
- the tenant is required to be a member for the duration of the term as are all other tenants.

(b) To repair

The tenant's repairing covenants must be carefully examined to ensure that:

- they are confined to clearly identified areas of the demised premises;
- only repairs as such are covered and not reinstatement or improvement;
- a clause is inserted to expressly exclude liability for structural defects. Where there is liability for structural repairs the covenant may be held to require the tenant to remedy inherent defects; see *Ravenseft Properties Ltd* v *Davstone (Holdings) Ltd* (1979);
- they are not unreasonable, taking into account the length of the lease and the age and condition of the property. Where the building is old advise the client to have a structural survey and have the report agreed with the landlord's surveyor. Because of the vulnerability of old property there should be a clause excluding liability for "fair wear and tear";
- if necessary try to protect the tenant by requiring a clause to provide for cesser of rent if the premises become unusable, and for determination of the lease if unusable for more than a reasonable period, unless the contingency is covered by insurance;
- the landlord's and tenant's specific repairing covenants together cover all works of repair likely to arise, including repair to the structure and common parts. (With a business tenancy, statute will not require the landlord to repair except perhaps if there is risk of injury to third parties.)

Repairing covenants must be considered with the covenants to insure, whether by landlord or by tenant, as there is a danger of the tenant being found liable for reinstatement if the risk is not covered by insurance.

If the tenant is to be responsible for all repairs in a modern building it would be wise to seek a covenant requiring the landlord to claim indemnity and if necessary take action against those responsible for the erection of the property should there be any structural defect.

(c) To insure

If the tenant is required to insure check that:

- the cover is adequate for the demised premises; it should be index-linked to cover all building costs;
- the building, if damaged or destroyed will have to be reinstated. If the landlord requires an option to determine the lease in the event of a total loss by fire, the landlord and not the tenant should undertake to insure;
- any block policy will cover the tenant's liability to other flat owners and third parties. In any case it would be wise for the client to have a supplemental policy to cover third party liability and to provide protection should the block policy lapse. The policy should cover also the tenant's own negligent acts;
- the client's mortgagee will be satisfied by the insurance provisions; he will not be if there is a clause causing the policy to be vitiated by the acts or omissions of owners of other flats or parts of the building.

A covenant to insure with a named company binds the tenant to take out the company's usual policy, even though it excludes some specific risks. The landlord will have the right to see the receipt for the last premium.

(d) User

Where the tenant of residential property is restricted to use as a private dwelling only, check that this meets his requirements, eg he may wish to take paying guests or use one room for business purposes.

With a business lease, the tenant should not agree to a restriction of use wider than that confining to a particular Use Class under Town and Country Planning legislation, as this should provide sufficient protection for the landlord. A restriction to one particular trade in a retail shop will place the tenant in a vulnerable position as regards competing trade, and may render the lease unmarketable. If there is to be such a restriction, the tenant should require the landlord not only to covenant not to let any adjoining premises he owns for competing business, but also to take action to enforce such covenants against adjoining tenants and to pay the costs of doing so; see *Rother* v *Colchester Corporation* (1969). Where change of use requires consent, it must be expressed that it will not be unreasonably refused, as this will not be implied.

Restrictions on the hours during which the premises can be used are unreasonable except where the letting is part of a building, and there are problems of security or provision of services. If there are such restrictions, they should be amended to permit use on certain occasions beyond the usual hours should the business so require, without there being a breach of covenant.

The user clause should be read in conjunction with the assignment clause, and failure to advise on the combined effect may amount to negligence; see *Sykes* v *Midland Bank Executor and Trustee Co Ltd* (1971).

Check that user is permitted under the Town and Country Planning Acts and under any superior lease or the freehold.

(e) Not to assign or sublet

A covenant restricting assignment, subletting, or otherwise dealing with the property may affect the value of the lease, and except in a short lease an absolute covenant would be unreasonable. There may be an absolute covenant against dealing with part of the premises, and a covenant not to part with the whole without the landlord's consent. As consent cannot be unreasonably withheld (see Landlord and Tenant Act 1927 s.19) this is generally acceptable unless the nature of the property is such that permission ought to be given to dispose of it in separate units. The tenant will then have a claim for damages if consent is unreasonably refused. It is wise to avoid the possibility of the landlord delaying consent by seeking to insert the words, "such consent must not be unreasonably withheld or delayed".

A clause requiring an offer to surrender the lease to the landlord before seeking to assign should be avoided if possible.

(f) Not to make alterations or improvements

The tenant of business premises may be prohibited from making alterations, additions, or improvements as these may attract compensation payments under the Landlord and Tenant Act 1927. Seek to modify an absolute prohibition to permit alterations with the landlord's consent. However, if the tenant should need to make alterations to comply with his statutory obligations, eg under the

Offices, Shops and Railway Premises Act 1963, and Factories Act 1961, the covenant can be suitably amended by the County Court.

4. Lessor's/landlord's covenants

(a) To insure

If the landlord is to insure it will usually be at the tenant's expense. There should be a requirement to reinstate the building if destroyed. This may not be possible if the insurance money is in sufficient to meet the claim, and the landlord may require an option to determine the lease rather than rebuild. In such a case the tenant should require a clause to provide compensation for any possible loss caused to the tenant's business. Both landlord and tenant would benefit from a provision apportioning the entitlement to insurance money should it prove impossible to reconstruct a badly damaged or demolished building. If the landlord is to insure by way of block policy, there should be some provision to enable the tenant to ascertain that the cover is sufficient and the policy has not been altered or lapsed.

If the landlord's covenant to insure is expressed to cover fire "and such risks as the landlord shall from time to time determine", risks such as storm or flood may not be covered. If the covenant is not widened to cover all potential damage, the tenant should be advised to take out his own policy to cover the risks omitted.

The landlord will usually claim the right to insure in "such office of repute as the landlord shall select". He is under no obligation to insure as inexpensively as possible.

There should be provision for the tenant to inspect any policy and endorsements to ensure that the terms will comply with the requirements of his mortgagee. The policy should be index-linked and related to the RICS scale of building costs. A mortgagee will require that the interests of the tenant and the mortgagee be endorsed on the policy on completion, and receipts for premiums paid must be produced on request. Problems can arise where the interests of a number of tenants are so endorsed. The insurer may refuse to pay on a claim until all persons named have signed. In a building sublet with parts frequently changing hands, this may be inconvenient and expensive.

The insurance covenant should be examined in conjunction with the tenant's repairing covenants.

(b) To repair

A landlord's covenant to keep the structure in repair should clearly identify what comprises the structure of the particular building, and

67

in a modern building should include responsibility for reinstatement even though the defects which may arise are the result of defective materials, negligent building methods, or faulty design.

The landlord's covenant to maintain the building or structure and exterior, at the tenant's expense, should impose a positive duty on the landlord to carry out works to a proper and reasonable standard, so that the building does not become dilapidated. In a business lease this could have an adverse effect on the tenant's customers and might possibly breach his statutory obligations to his employees. Check whether the tenant can have any control over the timing of repairs.

Although it will be implied that the tenant must give notice to the landlord of want of repair, it is wise to include this in the lease to bring it to his attention.

Ensure that the tenant will be able to enforce the covenant if the landlord fails to repair. In a block, if another tenant fails to repair, the landlord should be required to enforce the covenant, or have a duty and right of entry to carry out the necessary repair.

(c) To provide services

Services should be precisely defined. In the absence of an express provision, the Courts are reluctant to imply contractual obligation for the landlord to provide services. Usually there will be a clause exempting him from liability for failure to provide the services. Ensure that such exemptions refer specifically to causes beyond the landlord's control, and are not so wide as to serve as a defence for failure to provide services generally. Delete any provision which allows the landlord to alter the services during the term.

5. Provisos

(a) Re-entry

A provision that the lease will be forfeit on bankruptcy or liquidation will make it difficult for the tenant to obtain a mortgage advance. The landlord should be persuaded that there is sufficient protection under the tenant's covenants without this provision. He may be willing to accept a guarantor. A guarantor may wish to have an option to take over the lease if the tenant cannot pay the rent; this should be registered as an estate contract.

(b) Purchase of the reversion or renewal of the lease

If the lease gives the tenant the option to purchase the reversion or renew the lease ensure that there are adequate provisions in case of failure to reach agreement on the price or terms of the new lease.

6. Checklist

- Check the accuracy and spelling of names and addresses in contract and lease;
- Check that the contract is sound;
- Check that the property is adequately described in the parcels, that the plan agrees with the parcels and is referred to therein;
- Check that rights and easements, especially those relating to supply of services and rights of way, are precisely defined and are all that will be required;
- Have all required rights over common parts been granted?
- Ensure that any reservations by the lessor are reasonable;
- Is the date for commencement and length of term certain and as required by client?
- Is the rent as agreed between the parties and are payment dates certain? Is the rent review clause reasonable?
- Ensure that the tenant's covenants are reasonable having regard to the length of term;
- Ensure that landlord's services are precisely defined and that service charges are sufficient to cover the services, and are not unreasonable;
- Check that provisions for a sinking fund or tenants' company are comprehensive and fair, and that the tenant can participate in control of expenditure;
- Check that the tenant's repairing covenants refer precisely to the demised premises and are not unreasonable, bearing in mind the present state of repair. Look out for overlap or omissions in relation to other parts of the building;
- Check that the insurance covers all the demised premises and is for full reinstatement value including surveyor's and architect's fees;
- Check that restrictions on dealings and the use of the property are reasonable;
- Check permitted use under planning legislation;
- Examine landlord's covenants alongside tenant's covenants, particularly those relating to repair and insurance;

- Can landlord be required to enforce covenants against other tenants?
- Will all leases be in similar terms?
- Resist provisos for forfeiture on bankruptcy or liquidation;
- If appropriate, require an inventory of fixtures and fittings.

7. Replies to enquiries

Check carefully replies to enquiries and any entries revealed by the various searches and make further investigation if necessary; see Chapter 3.

8. Mortgage arrangements

If a mortgage is required check the mortgage arrangements. Ensure that the mortgagee is agreeable to the terms of the lease, and the mortgage advance will be available by the preferred date of completion; see Chapter 3.

If instructed to act for the purchaser's building society, acknowledge instructions (Appendix 2, Letter P6).

9. Approval of the draft lease or underlease and/or draft contract

When satisfied with replies to preliminary enquiries and searches, the draft lease may be amended to ensure that as far as possible there are no ambiguities or defects, and it is in accordance with client's instructions.

However, scope for amendment may be limited. In the case of a lease of a flat in a block, a house on an estate, or a suite of offices, it will have been provided that the lease is a standard one to which no amendments will be accepted. In the case of an underlease, scope for amendment will be restricted by the terms of any superior lease. When amendments are permitted, the draft may be returned marked "approved as amended in red". If there are fundamental alterations an explanation of the reasons in a letter accompanying the returned draft may assist.

The lessor's solicitor will have to decide which amendments can be accepted and which refused and will return the draft amended usually in green. If the parties cannot reach agreement at this stage, and particularly if the lessee's solicitor has given no reason for requiring his amendments, a meeting between solicitors would seem preferable to lengthy correspondence. If the reason for insertion or deletion of the various clauses is understood they may well be able to reach satisfactory agreement.

If the draft lease has been the subject of extensive amendments it will be safer to have the amended draft re-typed and checked. The altered original draft should be checked against the final version by the solicitors. Such examination will provide an appreciation of the total effect of the terms of the lease and give a last opportunity to ensure that the terms read as intended, comply with their clients' wishes, and that their interests are adequately protected. Ensure that clauses are correctly re-numbered consequent on amendment.

Check the terms of the draft contract. If satisfied, mark "approved", and return one copy attached to the draft lease, stating the matter is still "subject to contract".

When the terms of the lease and/or contract have been finally agreed, make a full report to the client on replies to preliminary enquiries, on searches, on enquiries of authorities, and on any observations arising from inspection of the property. Supply the client with a copy of the draft lease and explain carefully the terms, calling attention to unusual covenants and to his obligations under the lease, particularly with regard to payments he will have to make (Appendix 2, Letter P7).

10. Exchange of contracts

If there is to be no contract continue at Chapter 6.

If there is to be a contract, exchange must not take place until all financial arrangements have been made and any necessary mortgage offer has been received. When consents are necessary for the grant of a lease it is unwise to exchange contracts until these have been obtained. Confirm that the property will be covered by insurance from the moment of exchange. (Appendix 2, Letter P9). It is wise to call the client's attention to this important matter in writing.

Exchange procedure is discussed in Chapter 3.

Chapter 6

Between contract and completion

1. The abstract: vendor

On exchange of contracts evidence of title can be sent to the purchaser's solicitor at the same time as the vendor's part of the contract (Appendix 2, Letter V9). There will be, in any event, a time limit for delivery of the abstract stated in the contract.

In the case of registered title all that is required, if not already supplied, will be office copies of the entries on the Register; the filed plan and any documents noted on the Register; and an authority to inspect the Register.

If the title is unregistered there will have to be an abstract or epitome of title showing devolution from the contractual root of title to the present vendor's ownership. Every instrument which has affected or could affect the land must be abstracted except those referring only to interests or powers which will be overreached by the conveyance of the legal estate. In the case of an epitome ensure that the covering sheet sets out chronologically and in proper form the numbered instruments, their dates, the parties to the deeds or documents, and whether or not the original deed or document or an examined copy will be handed over at completion. Where the title deduced is partly by way of an abstract and partly by copy documents, the epitome should set out in sequence the details, as above, in respect of each abstracted dealing in order to show every link in the title. Plans should be carefully copied to show the appropriate colouring, and reveal T-marks, etc.

The vendor is bound to verify the abstract of title by producing the abstracted documents and he can be required to account for any documents not being in his possession. He is required to bear the cost of obtaining documents for preparation of the abstract and handing them over at completion.

Preparing an abstract or epitome should never be a hasty task so it is well to have had this in hand from the time of examining the deeds and drafting the contract. If using a previous abstract, mark any parts which refer to land not affecting the area now being sold.

Despite the ease of photocopying, every conveyancer should learn how to abstract to ensure that he can grasp the essentials of abstracts he will himself have to examine.

2. The purchaser/vendor situation

(a) Purchaser

On exchange of contracts the beneficial ownership passes to the purchaser. He has an estate contract which can be protected by registration; in the case of unregistered title as a Land Charge Class C(iv) against the name of the owner of the legal estate, and in the case of registered title by notice or by caution.

In practice the purchaser's interest is rarely registered unless there is likely to be delay in completion, but it has been stated that this practice should be reconsidered, particularly in view of the danger created by the Matrimonial Homes Act 1967; see Megarry J in *Wroth* v *Tyler* (1974).

The purchaser, as beneficial owner, will bear any losses of a capital nature insofar as such losses are not caused by breach of the vendor's duty to take reasonable care to preserve the property. Generally, the doctrine of frustration does not apply to contracts for the sale of land, so that a compulsory purchase order served after exchange of contracts but before completion will not enable the purchaser to rescind unless specifically provided for in the conditions of the contract.

The purchaser is entitled to gains of a capital nature which accrue to the land, but not to financial benefits not forming part of the contract.

(b) Vendor

Although after exchange of contracts the purchaser becomes the owner in equity, the vendor remains legal owner and may retain possession. The vendor is a qualified trustee to the extent that he must keep the property and any chattels included in the sale in sound condition and will be liable for damage which should have been prevented. He is not entitled to be indemnified for the cost of repairs. It may be otherwise if substantial improvements are necessary to prevent deterioraton, but the purchaser should be consulted. The vendor's duty extends to keeping agricultural land under proper cultivation, and his rights extend to gathering crops in the proper course of husbandry and retaining rents and profits up to completion.

The vendor will not be affected by notice to treat under a compulsory purchase order served between contract and completion; neither will he be affected by government intervention, as by listing the property as of historic or architectural interest unless there is a special condition in the contract. He will be liable for failure to give vacant possession at completion, even though this may be due to the act of a third party, eg a tenant holding over.

The vendor's duty to maintain the property lasts so long as he retains possession. If completion is delayed by the purchaser, the vendor is no longer under a duty and the purchaser will have no remedy.

A vendor who allows a purchaser into occupation before completion runs grave risks which need to be guarded against by a more carefully drawn clause than is usually found in standard conditions and the matter should be expressly provided for.

3. Requisitions on title

(a) Purchaser

On receipt of the abstract of title and within the time specified in the contract the purchaser's solicitor must raise requisitions on title (Appendix 2, Letter P11). These are questions or objections concerning the property contracted to be sold and the vendor's title thereto, and should be sent in duplicate in all cases, if only to obtain confirmation that the replies to preliminary enquiries are still complete and accurate. If another solicitor is acting for the purchaser's mortgagee an extra copy of the requisitions and replies will be needed for him, and he may also wish to raise his own requisitions. A standard form is normally used which covers matters such as: outgoings and apportionments, documents to be handed over on completion, discharge of subsisting mortgages, and completion arrangements. Questions should be inserted or amended as appropriate for the particular title, and irrelevant questions should be deleted.

The contract usually makes time of the essence for delivery of requisitions; this time limit does not include the day of delivery of the abstract. A condition in the contract limiting time will not apply to matters not discoverable from the abstract, eg arising out of Land Charges searches, nor will it apply to objections going to the root of title, nor to matters of "conveyance".

The purchaser's solicitor should not accept replies to requisitions unless they are given on the basis of the vendor's responsibility. It may be negligence to accept a reply from the vendor's solicitor such as, "so far as I am aware".

● *Unregistered title:* When the abstract is received it should be examined with the greatest care to trace an unbroken chain, from the root of title as provided for in the contract, to that of the vendor, free from incumbrances other than those subject to which the purchase is expressly being made. Notes should be drafted showing the continuity of title, marked to show the deeds and documents included in existing acknowledgements for production, correct stamp duty and mortgage redemption, any necessary land charges searches which have not been abstracted, and any queries on the title which should be raised. These notes will provide the draft for specific requisitions on title, a reminder of all the land charges searches yet to be made, and an outline for drafting the conveyance.

● *Registered title:* Requisitions will be needed on any matter not conclusive on the Register, particularly overriding interests which provide the greatest risk area in dealings with registered land. Requisitions will be necessary on any entry in the charges register which does not appear in the contract. If the title is less than absolute requisitions must be raised as though the land had unregistered title.

● *Assignment:* If the transaction is an assignment of an existing lease or underlease, requisitions on title should require production of the receipt for the last payment of rent due before the date of completion. Under the Law of Property Act 1925 s.45(2) on production of this receipt the purchaser shall assume that all the leasehold covenants and provisions have been observed and performed up to the date of completion.

(b) Vendor

The vendor is bound to answer all specific questions raised in respect of the property and his title thereto, unless expressly excepted from doing so by conditions in the contract (Appendix 2, Letter V11). Replies to requisitions are the vendor's responsibility, not that of his solicitor, and the replies should show they are made on that basis. Replies which appertain to the validity of the title need to be carefully drafted and any problem areas dealt with as thoroughly as though the replies were likely to be the subject of cross-examination. The trouble which can be caused by incomplete or inaccurate replies can vary from delay to court action for rescission of the contract.

See *Re Stone and Saville's Contract* (1963), which showed also that requisitions are necessary even though the title is registered. Where requisitions are improperly made out-of-time, the vendor's solicitor should state that his replies are made as a matter of courtesy and that contract time-limits are not thereby waived.

Most contracts make time of the essence for the purchaser's observations on the vendor's replies but, if these replies fail to answer satisfactorily any requisition, then it may be held that the vendor has effectively failed to reply and time will not run against the purchaser. The contract will give the vendor the right to rescind where he is unable or unwilling to comply with a requisition on title, but the vendor cannot rely on this right if he acts recklessly, unreasonably, or in bad faith. Where the requisition depends on "a matter of conveyance", not "a matter of title", the vendor cannot invoke the condition.

Check carefully the time limits specified in the contract relating to requisitions and the replies thereto, and the effect of delay, as standard form conditions vary.

- *Outgoings and apportionments:* Apportionments fall into three categories; those which can be calculated on completion, eg rent, rates; those which can only be accurately assessed after completion, eg repairs carried out by the landlord at the tenant's expense and accounts rendered half-yearly in arrears; and those which cannot be accurately apportioned, eg payments made in advance by a tenant to a maintenance fund. Where apportionments cannot be accurately assessed at completion a term in the contract could provide for a sum to be fixed and added to the contract price to avoid uncertainty. The Law Society's General Conditions allow for a provisional apportionment until the final amount is known.

  On completion the vendor must produce receipts for the last payment of outgoings of which either he claims reimbursement of an advance payment or arrears could be recovered from the purchaser. The vendor's solicitor should ask the vendor for the required receipts. If these are not available he should obtain confirmation of the amount and date of payment from the authority concerned, and an undertaking may be required from the vendor to pay any amounts due at completion. It is usual to inform rating authorities of the sale or grant, giving details of the property, completion date, and the purchaser. The authority will make the apportionment.

  If the property is being sold subject to a tenancy there will probably need to be an apportionment of rent and other payments received or receivable.

● *Completion statement:* Prepare an account of the amount required from the purchaser at completion. Give details of purchase price and deposit paid, and include any other payments required, eg apportioned outgoings (giving credit for payments made in arrears), chattels, fittings etc, and management company share, as included in the contract. State the net amount due, and the amounts to be allocated to your firm and to a bank, building society, etc. Send two copies to the purchaser's solicitor and retain a copy on file.

Confirm the arrangements regarding keys to be handed over at completion. These may be left with the vendor's solicitor or with the estate agent who on instructions will hand them to purchaser after completion.

4. Drafting the deed

It may not be possible to draft the deed until requisitions have been dealt with, but if there are no problems on the title the draft can be sent in duplicate to the vendor's solicitor for approval, with the requisitions on title, but subject to satisfactory replies thereto (Appendix 2, Letter P11). If another solicitor is acting for the purchaser's mortgagee, an extra copy of the draft must be supplied for his approval. In dealing with unregistered freehold a draft conveyance will be required; for unregistered leasehold a draft assignment; for registered land, whether freehold or leasehold, a draft transfer; for a draft lease or underlease see Chapter 4.

(a) Unregistered title

Use a good precedent when drafting the conveyance or assignment and follow it as closely as possible for the particular circumstances of the property being conveyed. For conveyances of parts of buildings or freehold flats, which involve complex provisions for cross easements and positive and negative covenants, reference should be made to a detailed work. Check that all necessary parties are included in the conveyance. The names should appear in full with the name of the purchaser placed last; ensure that the spellings are correct. Recitals should be as brief as possible but sufficient to provide the remedy of estoppel and give the benefit of the Law of Property Act 1925 s.45(6). Check that the parcels fully identify the property, especially if there have been boundary changes since the conveyance to the vendor, or a newly erected property changed from a plot number on an estate to a street number. If there is reference to a plan, insert one and require it to be signed by the parties. Do not use conflicting expressions, eg "delineated on the plan" and "by way of identification only" together. Normally plans show boundaries at ground level only, so take specific care if there is any sub-structure. If acting for joint purchasers ascertain that the draft carries out their intentions; joint tenancy or tenancy in common, as appropriate. Check that any indemnity clause for observance of restrictive covenants complies with the requirements of the contract and no more. Check that an acknowledgement for production, and undertaking for safe custody are included for deeds and documents not being handed over, and list these documents in a schedule. Insert a certificate of value appropriate to current legislation relating to stamp duty. Insert attestation clauses for the vendor; for the purchaser if entering into any covenants or if to hold jointly; and for any other party to the deed, eg the vendor's mortgagee if releasing the property from a mortgage security.

(b) Registered title

If the whole of the land in a registered title is being transferred it will be described as, "the land comprised in the title above-mentioned"; there will be no need for a plan, and a simple form of transfer will be used. Include an indemnity covenant as required by the contract, and if the transfer is to joint proprietors indicate how they are to hold; if as beneficial joint tenants the survivor can give valid receipt for capital money (Form 19; Form 19(Co) for transfer by a company or corporation; Form 19(JP) for transfer to joint proprietors). There are other forms for particular transactions.

Where part of the land in a title is being transferred, (Form 20, or Form 43 if new restrictive covenants are imposed), a plan based on the filed plan will be necessary, preferably coloured to conform with Land Registry usage. The plan must be signed by the transferor, or sealed if a limited company or corporation, and signed by or on behalf of the transferee. The filed plan identifies the land but does not delineate it; any conflict between the verbal particulars and the filed plan will be decided by the Registrar. It is possible to have the parties' own plan bound into the Land Certificate and even to replace the filed plan, but only where such plan is large-scale, detailed, and professionally drawn to deal with such matters as party walls or over-lapping floors.

The commonly used forms of transfer can be purchased in draft and engrossment form. In a simple transfer of whole where there are likely to be no queries, often the draft and engrossment are sent together for the vendor's solicitor's approval, with the appropriate seals affixed to the engrossment.

If the land has unregistered title but will be subject to compulsory registration on completion, the purchaser has a choice of using a conveyance or a transfer with title number left blank, and the property identified as comprised in a previous specified conveyance, mentioning the date and parties.

5. Final searches

Searches should be made a few days before completion, allowing sufficient time to check on any entries revealed, but allowing for advantage to be taken of the priority period after completion.

Companies search — When purchasing from a company, search in the Companies Register for charges or winding-up proceedings. As there will be no protection period the search should be made, usually by an agent, immediately before completion.

(a) Unregistered title

- *Land Charges search* — A search in the Register should be made against the names of all owners of the legal estate since 1925 where there are no existing search certificates. A search should be made against the vendor so that completion takes place during the period of protection; if completion is delayed the search must be repeated (Form K15). If acting for the purchaser's mortgagee a bankruptcy search should be made against the borrower (Form K16).

- *Local Land Charges search* — The search made before exchange of contracts should be repeated if there has been unusual delay.

- *Land Registry Parcels search* — Repeat the index search if in doubt as to the *bona fides* of the vendor.

(b) Registered title

If the title is less than absolute all searches appropriate to unregistered title as well as those appropriate to registered title need to be made.

- *Land Registry search* — A search in the Register should be made just prior to completion so that the purchaser has priority. If completion is delayed, a fresh search should be made so that the period of protection is extended. If acting in the purchaser's mortgage a search on behalf of the mortgagee will also cover the sale on which the mortgage will be dependent (Form 94A for whole of land in title, or Form 94B for part).

- *Land Charges search* — If acting for the purchaser's mortgagee a bankruptcy search should be made against the borrower (Form K16).
- *Local Land Charges search* — The search made before exchange of contracts should be repeated if there has been unusual delay as these charges constitute overriding interests in registered land.

6. Inspection of the property

Inspection should be arranged just before completion and enquiry made of anyone in occupation as to their interest in the property. In dealing with registered title the danger of such an occupier having an overriding interest makes inspection essential.

7. Bankruptcy before completion

A bankruptcy petition and the receiving order are both registered under the Land Charges Act 1972, whether or not the bankrupt is known to own land. If registered land appears to be affected, a creditors' notice of the petition and, when the receiving order is made, a bankruptcy inhibition, are entered against the title by the district land registry.

If the vendor becomes bankrupt before completion his duly appointed trustee in bankruptcy can enforce the contract. The trustee has the right to disclaim onerous property (see Bankruptcy Act 1914 s.54) but he cannot disclaim the contract so as to deprive the purchaser of his equitable interest, and specific performance could still be obtained.

If the purchaser becomes bankrupt before completion his trustee in bankruptcy can elect to adopt the contract or to disclaim it as unprofitable. If he does disclaim, the vendor can retain the deposit and he can prove in bankruptcy for any loss suffered by the disclaimer. He will however rank only as an ordinary unsecured creditor.

8. Death before completion

The death of either or both parties before completion does not affect the contract which remains enforceable.

If the vendor dies the contract is enforceable by, or against, the personal representatives upon whom the legal estate devolves. If the vendor was joint owner the survivor must proceed, and if he was a tenant for life selling settled land the Settled Land Act 1925, ss.63, 90 will apply. The contract will bind his successor in title who will have power to make dispositions to give effect to the contract. However, if on the death of the tenant for life the settlement comes to an end, the general personal representatives will complete the contract. In the case of registered land the personal representatives of a deceased vendor can transfer the legal estate without themselves being registered as proprietors; see Land Registration Act 1925, s.37 and Land Registration Rules 1925 r.170, although a purchaser can insist on the personal representatives first registering their own title.

If the purchaser dies before completion, the contract can be enforced by or against his personal representatives. As to the interest of persons beneficially entitled to the deceased's estate, and the liability to provide the balance of the purchase money, see Administration of Estates Act 1925, s.35.

9. Breach of contract

Choice of the most efficient remedy in the particular circumstances is important and often difficult.

If the purchaser fails to carry out his part of the contract, the standard form of contract will have imposed a term that the vendor may forfeit and retain the deposit and re-sell the property, claiming liquidated damages for any loss incurred. Under The Law Society Conditions the loss will include interest on the balance of the purchase money outstanding after the contractual completion date, giving credit for all sums received under the re-sale contract. The vendor can, alternatively, rely on his common law rights. Specific performance will not be granted to the vendor where his title to the property is doubtful, where there has been substantial misdescription in the contract, or where third-party rights would be prejudiced. Additionally, there are the usual equitable bars to relief such as delay or undue hardship to the other party. A Vendor and Purchaser Summons is a method of settling disputes on matters arising under the contract, other than its validity, but is not a suitable procedure for an order of specific performance.

Besides the usual remedies of rescission, specific performance and damages for breach of contract, it has been held that where a vendor wrongfully sells to a third party a purchaser may have a beneficiary's remedy "in *rem*" of "tracing" the land as trust property in its converted form of sale proceeds in the vendor-trustee's hands; see *Lake* v *Bayliss* (1974). Similarly a remedy of tracing in respect of breach of covenants for title against contributories of a dissolved company failed only because of the Companies (Winding Up) Rules 1949; see *Butler* v *Broadhead* (1975).

Chapter 7

Preparation for completion

In any sale and purchase of property there are so many items to be remembered and dealt with by both sides that it is unwise not to have attached to the file memoranda which can be implemented and checked. Prepare three lists — actions before completion; at completion; after completion. The completion list should include all deeds and documents to be dealt with at completion under the headings — inspect; obtain; hand over. Each item can be ticked when dealt with.

1. Purchaser/lessee

(a) Replies to requisitions on title

Check carefully and make any necessary observations on the vendor's replies within the contract time limit.

(b) Engrossment of the deed

The conveyance, transfer, or assignment, having been approved in draft by the vendor's solicitor should be engrossed, seals attached, and checked. If necessary it should be executed by the purchaser and attested before being sent to the vendor's solicitor in good time for execution by the vendor and any other parties to the deed (Appendix 2, Letter P12).

With a new lease, when the terms have been agreed, the lessor's solicitor will prepare an engrossment in duplicate and send the counterpart lease to the lessee's solicitor for the lessee to execute. If there is no contract, amendments to remedy some defective or onerous clause can still be called for after engrossment.

(c) Execution of the deed

It is preferable to request the client to visit your office to sign the various documents to avoid the possibility of mistake or postal delay

(Appendix 2, Letter P13). A transfer of registered land with a plan attached requires the plan to be signed by the transferor, and by or on behalf of the transferee, but in all cases The Law Society suggest that plans should be signed and clearly identified with the document that plan is annexed to. Any alterations must be initialled by the parties executing the deed and there must be no subsequent alterations or additions.

(d) Arrange mortgage advance

If acting for a building society or similar mortgagee send the report on title and request for cheque in good time to clear the cheque before completion (Appendix 2, Letter P14). The building society may provide its own printed form for this purpose. If the society sent a survey plan for identification of the parcels this will need to be returned with the report. Obtain the purchaser's execution of the mortgage deed, preferably in person and, if it is an endowment mortgage, the deed of assignment of the life policy. Obtain the policy and check it is in order (Appendix 2, Letter P15). Supply the purchaser with a copy of the building society rules and ensure that the mortgage covenants and clauses have been fully explained, eg letting and alterations to the mortgaged property will usually need prior consent of the mortgagee. If acting for a company borrowing on mortgage obtain a resolution of the board to borrow and to seal the mortgage, and prepare Form 395 for filing particulars of the charge at the Companies Registry within the prescribed period.

(e) Completion statement

Check from the vendor's completion statement that the amounts required on completion are accurate. Ensure that apportionments are dealt with equitably, particularly on an assignment where there is apportionment of maintenance and service charges, and where there may be outstanding claims not yet rendered but which refer to the period prior to completion.

(f) Completion arrangements

Check replies to requisitions and if completion is to be in person, note the time and place.

The money due on completion must be paid by the purchaser in accordance with the contract terms. The Law Society's General Conditions (1984) require this to be by 2.30 pm on the day of actual completion.

If completion is to be by post, and the vendor's solicitor has agreed to act as agent, send the same instructions as to any agent (Appendix 2, Letter P16). It is not possible to have completion by post if there is any conflict of interest, or if the mortgagee's instructions make this improper. If necessary appoint a solicitor in the town where completion is to take place.

If completion is to be by credit transfer, again the vendor's solicitor should be asked to complete as agent for the purchaser, so that responsibility lies on him. Check bank name, branch, and title and number of the account to be credited. If the respective accounts are not with the same bank, or if there is a concurrent sale and purchase, bear in mind the delays that can occur and consider using a specialised service such as the Trustee Savings Bank "Speedsend" service or the Clearing House Automated Payments System (CHAPS).

If the completion money is to be paid by banker's draft arrange this with your bank after checking requisitions to see whether more than one draft is required: if so, in whose favour and for what amounts.

(g) Chattels

If chattels, fittings, etc are being purchased, send a receipt to be signed by the vendor and handed back on completion.

(h) Deposit

If the deposit is being held by an estate agent or perhaps an auctioneer as stakeholder, prepare a letter of release to be handed to the vendor's solicitor at completion.

(i) Keys

Check the arrangements made for the keys to be handed to the purchaser on completion.

(j) Bill of costs

Prepare the bill of costs and completion statement for the client, showing in detail receipts and payments made, and due to be made after completion. Request a cheque for the balance as required, in time for clearance before completion.

2. Vendor/lessor

Prepare lists — actions before completion; at completion; after completion, to ensure that no matter is overlooked.

(a) Approval and execution of the deed

Check and return the draft conveyance, transfer, or assignment, marked "approved as drawn", or "approved as amended in red", to the purchaser's solicitor for engrossment. Any slips in drafting to the purchaser's disadvantage should be amended as a matter of courtesy.

The engrossment, when received from the purchaser's solicitor, is ready for execution by the vendor and any other party to the deed.

With a new lease, when the terms have been agreed the lessor's solicitor prepares the engrossment. Two copies are made, the lease and counterpart lease; they should be well presented and securely bound with firm covers. The counterpart is sent to the lessee's solicitor for execution and the lease to the lessor for execution (Appendix 2, Letter V11).

Wherever possible request the client to visit your office to sign the various documents, explaining each before signature. If deeds have to be sent by post enclose instructions on how to execute (Appendix 2, Letter V12).

(b) Escrow

When the deed is signed and sealed and handed to the client's solicitor it has been delivered in escrow conditional on performance of some requirement, eg payment of the premium or purchase money. Even destruction of the seal and removal of signature will not prevent the escrow becoming a binding deed once the condition has been fulfilled; see *Vincent* v *Premo Enterprises (Voucher Sales) Ltd* (1969). This is so despite an arrangement that the deed should be executed in duplicate and the two deeds exchanged; see *Kidner* v *Keith* (1863).

Delay in completion of the transaction will not prevent the escrow from becoming a deed on payment of the purchase monies; see *Kingston* v *Ambrian Investments Co Ltd* (1975).

The dangers attendant on sealing of deeds in escrow must be borne in mind. If, for example, a lease or counterpart is sealed before all matters have been finally agreed, clear evidence must exist that the sealing was conditional.

The date from which rent is payable may relate back to the date of delivery of a lease as an escrow even though the lessee does not have possession until much later; see *Alan Estates Ltd* v *W G Stores Ltd* (1981). Hence, if there are any items not yet finalised, it must be made clear beyond doubt that the sealing is conditional on particular matters being determined; even so there may be danger that a court may hold that a particular condition did not prevent a deed being binding; see *Beesly* v *Hallwood Estates Ltd* (1961).

(c) Discharge of mortgage

If the property is in mortgage write to the mortgagee quoting the reference or roll number, stating the contractual completion date, and requesting a redemption statement and details of interest to be charged should there be an unforeseen delay in completion (Appendix 2, Letter V13). Many building societies provide a daily rate of interest to apply after a given redemption date, and others provide a figure which remains firm throughout the whole month during which it is expected redemption will take place.

Prepare as far as possible the relevant discharge. An unregistered title will require the statutory receipt on the mortgage deed. If there is a *puisne* mortgage or equitable charge registered on the land charges register, an application for cancellation will be needed (Form K11). In the case of registered title Land Registry Form 53 will be required, or a bank's own version of Form 53; or Withdrawal of Notice of Deposit; or where the property forms part only of a mortgagee's security a letter or form of consent to dealing.

If the mortgage is an endowment mortgage prepare the re-assignment of the life policy. Where the vendor is a limited company and a mortgage was entered into prior to 1 January 1970, or there is a floating charge of any date, these will have been registered in the Companies Register. Prepare the relevant company form for execution by a director and the secretary.

(d) Undertakings

Prepare any necessary undertakings to be given at completion. If there is any doubt as to the undertaking required discuss the matter with the purchaser's solicitor. The undertakings should be ready for the vendor to sign when he executes the deed.

The Law Society regard the failure by a solicitor to honour an undertaking as a breach of professional conduct *(Law Society's Guide to the Professional Conduct of Solicitors,* p.67–71). Hence the solicitor should never give an undertaking on behalf of his client unless he can personally ensure its implementation. The possibility of the client becoming bankrupt should be borne in mind. The danger arises, not with the carefully worded undertaking prepared in advance, but with some unforeseen matter arising on completion.

If the property is in mortgage, prepare an undertaking to redeem the mortgage and to send the receipted mortgage, or if registered, the sealed/signed Land Registry Form 53, to the purchaser's solicitor as soon as received from the mortgagee. The Law Society have approved a form of undertaking in respect of building society mortgages but not other mortgages (Appendix 2, Letter V14).

(e) Schedule of title deeds

Prepare in triplicate (2 for the purchaser, 1 for the file) a schedule of deeds and documents to be handed over at completion, checking against the abstract or epitome.

(f) Completion arrangements

Completion usually takes place at the office of the vendor's solicitor or the vendor's mortgagee's solicitor. Completion by post is approved by The Law Society so long as the proper procedure is adopted; in this case the vendor's solicitor must have agreed to act as agent usually without expectation of an agency fee.

(g) Estate agent's account

Obtain and check the estate agent's account for commission on the sale. Send a copy of the account to the vendor requesting him to confirm that the rate being charged is as agreed, and that you are authorised to pay the account on completion from the sale proceeds.

(h) Chattels

Check the position regarding any chattels, fittings, etc being sold, and check the receipt required by the purchaser. Obtain the vendor's signature when he calls to execute the other documents.

(i) Share transfer

Where a management company share is to be transferred to the purchaser check the share certificate and prepare a stock transfer form to be handed over with the share certificate at completion.

(j) Notice to tenant

If the property is being sold subject to a tenancy prepare an authority addressed to the tenant to be handed over on completion authorising him to pay future rents to the purchaser or to his agent.

(k) Keys

Check with the vendor the arrangements regarding keys to be handed over at completion.

(l) Bill of costs

Prepare the bill of costs and a completion statement showing in detail payments, receipts, and the balance due to or from the client.

Chapter 8

Completion and after

1. Introduction

Completion, in the absence of any condition to the contrary, means "the complete conveyance of the estate and final settlement of the business"; see *Killner* v *France* (1946). Generally the contract merges into the conveyance, and all rights under the contract are extinguished unless other intention has been shown. Thus, once completion has taken place it will usually be too late for claims unless the existence of a collateral contract can be shown which has not been satisfied. However, where a contract provides for vacant possession but part of the property is found on completion to be occupied, it appears that the contract will not have merged into the conveyance and damages will lie for breach; see *Hissett* v *Reading Roofing Co Ltd* (1970).

The vendor's solicitor must be ready to hand over to the purchaser's solicitor all agreed deeds and documents on completion or provide an undertaking in lieu, and to produce for examination deeds and documents not being handed over, eg deeds which refer to land being retained by the vendor, or a Grant of Probate or Letters of Administration. If there are retained deeds or documents, the vendor's solicitor should be ready to endorse on these an agreed memorandum of the sale and an acknowledgement for production of the relevant deed or document.

In the case of registered title where part only of the land in the title is being sold the vendor's solicitor should deposit the land or charge certificate at the appropriate district land registry to await the pending dealing and, at or before completion, give the purchaser's solicitor the deposit number. If the certificate has not yet been deposited, give an undertaking to do so and to supply the deposit number when known.

The vendor's solicitor should hand over the conveyance, assignment, or transfer with the date of completion inserted. A "made-up" copy should be retained on file. Completion of the grant of a lease or underlease is effected by the lessor's solicitor handing over the executed lease in exchange for the sealed counterpart with dates inserted in all relevant parts.

Before handing over the completion money the purchaser's solicitor must check the title deeds and documents against the abstract or epitome, and check that all other documents are in order. On assignment, the lease or underlease must be handed over.

The balance of the purchase monies, including any necessary apportionments, will be paid as agreed to the vendor/lessor by way of banker's draft or by credit transfer (Appendix 2, Letters P16, P17). The vendor's solicitor must check that this amount agrees with his completion statement.

If the deposit or any part of it is held by a third party as stakeholder, the vendor will require a letter from the purchaser's/lessee's solicitor authorising its release.

If there is delay in completion, compensation may be required from the party in default. The standard forms of contract provide alternative remedies, and the general and special conditions, and contract interest rate should be carefully checked.

If the purchaser goes into occupation before completion, standard form conditions provide for payment of interest, expenses, etc.

2. Completion checklist: vendor/lessor

- Retain made-up copy of conveyance, assignment or transfer;
- Check all dates have been inserted in counterpart lease and that it has been properly executed;
- Obtain receipted copy of schedule of title deeds;
- Ensure that no extraneous documents are handed over, eg deed of assignment of life policy;
- Check completion money, including any apportionments, against completion statement;
- Obtain deposit release if required;
- Following completion by post or credit transfer, write to the purchaser's solicitor; acknowledge completion monies, confirm completion, enclose deeds, documents, and schedule (Appendix 2, Letter V15).

3. Completion checklist: purchaser/lessee

- Check that no dates have been omitted from the conveyance, assignment, transfer or lease, and that the deed has been property executed;

- If there are retained deeds or documents check that a memorandum of the sale and an acknowledgement for production is endorsed thereon;
- If part of the land in registered title is being purchased obtain the Land Registry deposit number;
- Obtain an undertaking for any documents to be supplied subsequently;
- Obtain an undertaking to discharge the mortgage and to forward the mortgage deed with vacating receipt or Form 53 for registered title;
- Obtain any necessary cancellations of land charge entries, or obtain certification on the land charges search certificate that any particular entry does not affect the land being purchased;
- Check apportionments, receipts for outgoings or undertakings to pay any amounts due if receipts are not available;
- If the property is subject to a tenancy ensure that an authority directed to the tenant to pay future rent to the purchaser is handed over;
- If required, obtain the management company share certificate and transfer form;
- Obtain the vendor's receipt for chattel money;
- If vacant possession is being given check that all keys are handed over.

4. After completion: vendor

(a) Mortgage

Ensure that all mortgages are discharged as at completion date and any registrations cancelled. Immediately after completion send to the mortgagee the amount required to redeem the mortgage, with the mortgage deed or Form 53 (Appendix 2, Letter V16). When the receipted mortgage deed, or signed/sealed Form 53, is returned, check that the correct date has been inserted and forward it to the purchaser's solicitor in compliance with the undertaking (Appendix 2, Letter V17).

(b) Undertaking to bank

If an undertaking has been given to the client's bank, the balance of the purchase monies in hand should be remitted without delay as required by the undertaking together with a request for confirmation that this undertaking is thereby discharged.

(c) Deposit

Send the deposit release to the deposit holder requesting payment of the deposit to you.

(d) Life policy

Arrange for re-assignment of the life policy if an endowment mortgage is redeemed, and notify the insurer (Appendix 2, Letter V18). When the policy has been re-assigned place the deed with the policy and send them to the client.

(e) Estate agent

If so instructed by the client, pay the estate agent's account, or if he is holding a deposit, request the balance after deducting his commission (Appendix 2, Letter V19). Check the amounts.

(f) Report to client

Report on completion and send a statement of account together with the receipted bill of costs, the amount thereof having previously been agreed. Send a cheque for the balance due, or invest the proceeds as instructed. All cheques sent by post should be crossed and, if the client has a bank account, marked "account payee only" for safety. Remind the client to cancel the insurance on property sold, and apply for any refund of premium due (Appendix 2, Letter V20).

5. After completion: purchaser/lessee

(a) Mortgage

Check the purchaser's mortgage deed bears the same date as the conveyance, assignment, transfer or lease, and that all blanks in the deed are completed. Report on completion to the mortgagee (Appendix 2, Letter P18).

In the case of a mortgage of a life assurance policy give notice to the insurer in duplicate of assignment of the policy and, when returned, file the receipted copy of the notice with the policy (Appendix 2, Letter P19).

If acting for a company, file particulars of any mortgage or charge with the Companies Registry within 21 days.

(b) Notices: leasehold

Serve any notices required under the terms of the lease or any superior lease in respect of the assignment or mortgage and pay the required fee, obtain an acknowledgement and place it with the deeds (Appendix 2, Letter P20). Retain a file copy.

Serve any notices on insurers as required under the lease. Obtain an acknowledgment and place it with the deeds (Appendix 2, Letter P21). Retain a file copy.

(c) Options: leasehold

If the lease contains an option to purchase or renew, this should be protected immediately by registration as an estate contract; in unregistered title as a Land Charge Class C (iv), or in registered title by way of notice.

(d) Report to client

Report on completion and submit a statement of account. If the client will not be receiving the title deeds, eg if they are to be held by a mortgagee, ensure that he has a copy of the mortgage and, if leasehold, a copy of the lease or summary of the leasehold terms, or if freehold, a copy of any restrictive covenants affecting the property (Appendix 2, Letter P22).

(e) Stamp duty

Send the deed to the Stamp Office with the duty payable; retain a made-up copy on file.

It is important to check current regulations for changes in procedure and rates of duty.

(f) Vendor's redeemed mortgage

When received, check that the vendor's redeemed mortgage deed/Form 53 bears a date not later than the day of completion. Confirm that the undertaking of the vendor's solicitor is now discharged.

(g) Registration

If the title requires first registration or is already registered, a completed application form must be submitted with the required documents and fee to the appropriate district land registry. There are numerous land registration application forms, and it is essential that the correct form is used for the particular transaction. Choice of form will depend on whether the application is:

- for first registration or for dealings with a registered title;
- for dealing with the whole or part of the land in the registered title;
- on behalf of a company or corporation;
- for freehold or leasehold title;
- for absolute or lesser title, if leasehold.

For example:

Where land has registered title, complete Form A4 for dealings with the whole of the land in title, and Form A5 for dealings with part. For first registration of freehold land on behalf of a recent purchaser other than a company or corporation Form 1B must be submitted with Form A13 in triplicate.

On the grant of new lease or underlease:

(i) if the lessor's title is registered, application for first registration of a term granted for more than 21 years must be made whether or not the land is in an area of compulsory registration;

(ii) if in an area of compulsory registration, a term of not less than 40 years must be registered;

(iii) if in an area of compulsory registration, a term of more than 21 years or having more than 21 years to run may be registered, whether or not the reversion is registered.

When acting for a public sector tenant purchasing under the provisions of the Housing Act 1980 the title must be registered whether leasehold or freehold, irrespective of whether the property is in an area of compulsory registration.

Registration checklist:

- Check all deeds are in order with dates and particulars inserted;
- Check that copy documents have been correctly certified;
- Choose the correct application form and ensure that it is fully completed and signed;
- Enclose all the required documents and the correct fee, and

ensure that all other requirements are satisfied. Failure to do so will cause delay, and the Registrar may find it necessary to raise requisitions.

Application for registration of a dealing in registered land must be made within the search priority period. Application for first registration must be made within two months of completion.

On receipt of the documents from the Land Registry after registration, carefully examine the land or charge certificate to ensure that it is correct in every detail, and check that the documents not to be retained by the Registrar have been returned.

(h) Management company

If there has been a transfer of a management company share attend to registration.

(i) Title deeds

If sending title deeds to a mortgagee prepare extra copies of the schedule, one to be receipted and returned by the mortgagee, and one for the purchaser to retain. When the title is registered, a building society may wish to have only essential pre-registration documents, and if there are old deeds the client may like to have them. If the property is not in mortgage check with the client whether the deeds are to be sent to a bank for safekeeping.

Appendix 1

Specimen instruction sheets

Sale or purchase of freehold/leasehold

Ref.	Preferred date of completion	Name of client
Date	Concurrent sale and purchase yes/no	

SALE/PURCHASE as: —   — REGISTERED/UNREGISTERED   FREEHOLD/LEASEHOLD property known

Price £	Deposit £ paid to	Vacant possession YES/NO

Deeds with	Local Authority

Client   VENDOR/PURCHASER   SOLE/JOINT TENANTS/TENANTS IN COMMON
Name(s) —
—
Address —
—
—
Telephone — HOME   WORK

Other Party   Name —
Solicitor   Name —   Ref.
Address —
—
—
Telephone —

Estate Agent   Name —
Address —
—
Telephone — | Agent's circular received

Survey arrangements

| | Year property built |

Mortgage   TO BE ARRANGED/REDEEMED

Insurance arrangements   PROPERTY   LIFE

Fixtures etc to be included

Other items

Grant of a new lease/underlease

Date	Ref.	Grant of new LEASE/UNDERLEASE	Client

Details of property	Premium £	Term	Commencement date

Rent (amount, dates) —
Rent review   *Rates* —

Rights
To be granted —
To be reserved —

Repairs and Maintenance
Landlord —
Tenant —
Present state —

Services
Payment for —
Management company —

Insurance
Landlord —
Tenant —

Use
Existing —
Proposed —

Third party interests

Costs

Consents

References

Other items

Appendix 2

Model letters

A model letter should be regarded as a starting point from which an inexperienced conveyancer may draft his own letter to suit the circumstances of the particular transaction. Simple "covering" letters are not included, nor are those letters which can be drafted by reference to the text. An oblique stroke in a model letter indicates alternative words or phrases; a bracket indicates material not directly forming part of the letter.

All letters should bear the date, references of the sender and recipient, and be headed by the address of the property. Ensure that names and addresses are correctly spelled; refer to previous communication by letter or telephone with date, and to documents received or enclosed.

It is good conveyancing practice and a matter of courtesy to send additional copies of documents for the convenience of the solicitor acting for the other party.

If requesting the client to reply to a letter or to return documents, enclose a suitable stamped addressed envelope.

1. Acting for Vendor/lessor

V1 To client confirming instructions

Thank you for your instructions with regard to the sale/lease of your freehold/leasehold property for the price/premium of £....
We shall be pleased to act on your behalf.

Please let us have the title deeds or, if the property is in mortgage, the name, address, and the reference or roll number of the mortgagee holding the deeds.

When these have been examined we will prepare the draft contract and/or draft lease for the approval of the purchaser's/lessee's solicitor.

(Set out in separate paragraphs any special instructions you have been given and the terms of any undertaking your client has authorised. If acting on the grant of a new lease, outline the proposed terms.)

The transaction will remain, "subject to contract", enabling you or the purchaser to withdraw at any time until contracts are exchanged, then you will both be bound by the contract terms. This we will explain when the contract is ready for you to sign.

We shall make every endeavour to adhere to your preferred completion date of *(date)*.

V2 To purchaser's solicitor making initial contact

Subject to Contract/Lease

We act for *(name of client)* on the proposed sale/lease of the above freehold/leasehold property for £... / for a term of ... years at an initial rent of £... per annum, subject to contract/lease.

We understand that you act for the purchaser/lessee *(name and address)*, and as soon as the title deeds are to hand we will submit a draft contract and/or draft lease to you for approval.

We enclose a suitable plan for the purpose of your local search. The local authority is ....

V3 To mortgagee requesting title deeds

Property ....
Borrower ....
Roll number ....

Our client *(name)* is proposing to sell/lease the above property which is in mortgage to your Society.

In order that we may prepare a draft contract/lease will you please send the title deeds to us.

We undertake to hold the deeds on behalf of the Society on the usual undertaking to return the deeds on demand or to arrange for the mortgage to be repaid.

(If acting on the grant of a new lease, and the mortgagee's consent is required, request this and outline the proposed terms of the lease.)

V4 To estate agent requesting particulars

We are acting for *(name of client)* on the sale/lease of the above property, subject to contract/lease. We will submit a draft contract and/or lease to the solicitor acting for the purchaser/lessee as soon as the title deeds are to hand.

In the meantime will you please let us have details of your agency agreement with our client and of any reservation fee or preliminary deposit paid by the purchaser.

Please also provide us with a copy of your sale particulars relating to the property.

V5 To purchaser's solicitor with draft contract/lease

Further to our letter of *(date)* we now enclose a draft contract and/or draft lease for your approval, with a copy for your use. We also enclose office copy entries on the Register, documents noted and filed plan/copies of the restrictive covenants referred to/a copy of the lease under which the property is held.

We look forward to hearing from you.

(In dealing with a building estate, refer to and enclose: replies to standard preliminary enquiries together with the required documents, eg copy of planning permission, bye-law or building regulation consent; documentation as to the vendor's title; and draft conveyance/transfer. Indicate that amendments cannot be permitted.)

V6 To client to check replies to preliminary enquiries

We have submitted a draft contract to your purchaser's solicitor and have received from him the enclosed enquiries. We have entered replies to most of the questions from the information on hand, and we shall be grateful if you will insert replies to those questions marked which we have been unable to answer.

Will you please then go through and check carefully that all of the answers are accurate, and indicate any corrections needed before returning the form to us.

V7 To purchaser's solicitor returning preliminary enquiries

Thank you for your letter of *(date)* enclosing your preliminary enquiries, we are grateful for the additional copy.

We enclose our replies thereto, which we have checked with our client, and we shall be pleased to receive your approval of the draft contract and/or lease.

V8 To client regarding signing of contract/approving the lease

The terms of the contract and/or lease have now been agreed with the purchaser's/lessee's solicitor and we shall be pleased if you will contact us to arrange an appointment at a time convenient to you to discuss the matter/sign the contract.

(If the matter has to be dealt with by post) The terms of the contract and/or lease have now been agreed with the purchaser's solicitor and we enclose the contract for you to sign where indicated/the draft lease for your approval.

(Explain the contract terms and/or terms of the lease as necessary, and the rights and obligations of both parties following exchange if there is to be a contract.)

If you will then return the signed contract/approve the draft lease, we will proceed to exchange after a completion date has been agreed. We understand that the purchaser wishes to complete and move into the property on *(date)*. Please confirm that this is acceptable to you, or, if not, let us have an alternative date.

V9 To purchaser's solicitor exchanging contracts

Thank you for your letter of *(date)* enclosing the part of the contract signed by your client, and a cheque for the deposit of £... to be held by us as stakeholders. We have inserted today's date, and the completion date *(date)* as agreed on both parts of the contract and we enclose the part signed by our client by way of exchange.

We also enclose the abstract of title, and we shall be pleased to receive the draft conveyance/assignment for approval./

As the title is registered we hereby authorise you, on behalf of our client, to inspect the Register. We shall be pleased to receive the draft transfer for approval./

We are arranging for the lease and counterpart to be engrossed and will forward the counterpart to you as soon as possible for execution by your client.

V10 To client confirming exchange of contracts

We are pleased to confirm that contracts have been exchanged for the sale/lease of your property in accordance with your instructions.

Completion has been arranged for *(date)* as agreed, when you will be required to give vacant possession *(not if sold subject to a tenancy)*.

We will contact you again when the completion documents are ready for you to sign.

V11 To purchaser's solicitor with replies to requisitions and draft deed/ counterpart lease

Thank you for your letter of *(date)* enclosing your requisitions on title and the draft conveyance/assignment/transfer. We are grateful for the additional copies.

We enclose replies to your requisitions and the draft conveyance/assignment/ transfer approved as drawn/amended.

(If necessary explain why draft has been amended.)

or

Thank you for your letter of *(date)* enclosing your requisitions on title. We are grateful for the additional copy.

We enclose replies to your requisitions and the counterpart lease for execution by your client.

(Replies to requisitions are the vendor's responsibility and if there is any element of doubt the replies should first be checked with the client.)

V12 To client regarding execution of the deed

The documents have now been prepared in readiness for completion. We shall be pleased if you will contact us to arrange an appointment at a time convenient to you to obtain your signature and discuss the completion arrangements.

(If the matter has to be dealt with by post:) We enclose the following documents for you to sign in readiness for completion.

(List all documents, explain the various clauses in the deed as necessary and point out the consequences of delivery of the deed as an escrow.)

Will you please sign the deed where indicated, in the presence of an adult witness who is not a party to the deed, and who should then add his or her name, address, and occupation also where indicated.

We also enclose copies of the estate agent's account and the mortgagee's redemption statement. Will you please check these, and if you have any queries let us know as soon as possible. We shall assume, unless we hear from you to the contrary, that you wish us to pay the estate agent's account for you from the sale proceeds on completion.

Please arrange with the respective authorities to clear the general, water, and sewerage rates up to the completion date, and let us know the arrangements you wish to make with regard to the keys. We suggest you leave these with the estate agent, and we will authorise release to the purchaser on completion. We take this opportunity of enclosing our bill of costs and disbursements which, with your agreement, we will include in the final statement of account. It will be helpful if you will return the signed deed and documents to us as soon as possible.

V13 To building society requesting redemption statement

Property . . . .
Borrower . . . .
Roll number . . . .

Further to our letter of *(date)* concerning the proposed sale of the above property, contracts have now been exchanged with the completion date agreed as *(date)*. Will you please notify us of the redemption figure for this date and the daily interest rate thereafter in case of delay.

V14 Undertaking to discharge mortgage

Re: . . . .

In consideration of your today completing the purchase of *(address of property)*, we hereby undertake forthwith to pay over to *(name of building society)* the money required to redeem the mortgage/legal charge dated . . . . , and to forward the receipted mortgage/legal charge/signed/sealed Form 53 to you as soon as it is received by us from the Society.

(This undertaking is based on the form recommended by The Law Society for building society mortgages, but see J. E. Adams, Law Society's Gazette, 1980, Vol.77(10), p.259, for suggested amendments.)

V15 To purchaser's solicitor following completion by post or credit transfer

We acknowledge receipt of the completion monies of £ . . . . , and we confirm that the transaction has been completed today as arranged.

We enclose the conveyance/assignment/transfer/lease, and the title deeds and documents as listed in the schedule.

We also enclose our undertaking to discharge the mortgage and *(ensure that all documents enclosed are referred to, eg share certificate, receipt for chattel money, authority addressed to tenant)*. Please acknowledge receipt and sign and return one copy of the schedule.

V16 To building society with redemption money

Property ....

Borrower ....

Roll number ....

We refer to your redemption statement dated ....
and confirm that the sale of the property was completed today.

We enclose our cheque for £ .... , being the amount
required to redeem the mortgage as at today's date. We also enclose
the mortgage deed/legal charge/Form 53, and we shall be grateful if
you will arrange for the receipt/Form to be sealed by the Society and
returned to us as soon as possible.

As the life policy was also in mortgage we enclose the deed, please
arrange for the re-assignment to be sealed.

Please cancel the insurance on the property, and forward to us any
refund of premium due.

V17 To purchaser's solicitor regarding discharged mortgage

We now enclose the receipted mortgage/Form 53 and we shall be
grateful if you will confirm that our undertaking in this respect is
now discharged.

V18 To vendor's insurance company giving notice of re-assignment of life policy

Life assured ....

Policy number ....

We hereby give notice that by a re-assignment dated .... ,
made between *(name of building society)* and *(life assured)*, the
above-mentioned policy was re-assigned to *(name)*, the assured.

V19 To estate agent settling account

We are pleased to confirm that the sale of the above property has
been completed. We have been instructed to settle your account, and
accordingly we enclose a cheque for £ ....

Will you please receipt and return the copy of your account which is
also enclosed.

V20 To client confirming completion

We are pleased to confirm that the sale was completed today as
arranged, and we received the sum of £ ....

You will see from the enclosed completion statement that we have paid £ .... to the *(name of building society)* being the amount required to redeem your mortgage, and we have settled the estate agent's account, as instructed. We have deducted our costs, for which we thank you, and enclose the receipted account. We enclose a cheque for the balance due to you of £ ....
(If other instructions have been received confirm in detail that they have been complied with.)

We have arranged for the insurance on the property to be cancelled and will forward to you any refund of premium received. We have also requested that your life policy which was in mortgage to the building society be re-assigned to you. We will forward the policy and the discharged mortgage, when received, for you to retain.

2. Acting for Purchaser/Lessee

P1 To client confirming instructions

Thank you for your instructions with regard to the purchase/lease of the above freehold/leasehold property for the price/premium of £ ....
We shall be pleased to act on your behalf.
(Set out in separate paragraphs any special instructions you have been given and, if acting on the grant of a new lease, the terms required. Mention the proposed mortgage arrangements and refer to the deposit which will be required. Detail the terms of any undertaking your client has authorised.)

We have written to the vendor's/lessor's solicitor requesting a draft contract and/or draft lease, and will put in hand the necessary searches and enquiries.

The transaction will remain, 'subject to contract', enabling you or the vendor to withdraw at any time until contracts are exchanged, then you will both be bound by the contract terms. This we will explain when the contract is ready for you to sign.

We shall make every endeavour to adhere to your preferred completion date of *(date)*.

If you have any queries please do not hesitate to contact us.

P2 To vendor's solicitor requesting draft contract/lease
Subject to Contract/Lease
We act for *(name and address of client)* on the proposed purchase/lease of the above freehold/leasehold property for
£ .... /for a term of .... years at an initial rent of
£ .... per annum, subject to contract/lease.

We understand that you act for the vendor/lessor *(name)* and we shall be pleased to receive a draft contract and/or draft lease for approval. *(Request a copy of the lease if purchasing an existing lease.)*

We shall be grateful if you will supply us with a plan suitable for the purpose of our local search.

P3 To estate agent requesting particulars

We are acting for *(name of client)* on the purchase/lease of the above freehold/leasehold property, subject to contract/lease, and we understand that you have arranged the sale on behalf of the vendor. Please provide us with a copy of your sale particulars relating to the property, and let us have the name and address of the solicitor acting for the vendor.

P4 To client to check draft contract/lease

We have received the draft contract and/or draft lease from the vendor's/lessor's solicitor, and we shall be pleased if you will contact us to arrange an appointment at a time convenient to you to discuss the matter.

P5 To vendor's/lessor's solicitor with preliminary enquiries
Subject to contract/lease

Thank you for your letter of *(date)* enclosing the draft contract and/or draft lease. We are grateful for the additional copies. We return herewith the draft(s) approved as drawn/amended, subject to satisfactory replies to the enclosed preliminary enquiries and to our local search and enquiries.

(Make the approval subject also to any other outstanding matter.)

P6 To building society acknowledging instructions

Property ....
Borrower ....
Roll number ....

We thank you for your instructions regarding the proposed mortgage of the above property. We shall be pleased to act on behalf of the Society, and we will notify you as soon as contracts have been exchanged.

P7 To client with report on contract/lease

We have now completed the preliminary enquiries and searches and

enclose the following documents for you to examine:
(List all documents enclosed, eg
1. *the contract and/or draft lease*
2. *copy of the existing lease if there is to be an assignment*
3. *copy of restrictive covenants*
4. *preliminary enquiries with replies*
5. *local searches and enquiries)*

As you will see the documents are quite detailed and we call your attention particularly to the following:

(Deal with each document separately, eg contract — *draw attention to such matters as description of the property, effect of any restrictions, proposed completion date, contract interest rate;* lease — *duration, rent, service charge, repairs and maintenance, any unusual clauses;* preliminary enquiries — *boundaries, disputes, services, items included, rateable value;* local searches and enquiries — *road works, drainage, tree preservation orders, plannng permission, future plans for the area, whether registration of title needed. Refer to the need for a survey before exchange, the mortgage arrangements and any conditions imposed by the mortgagee, and insurance required on exchange.)*

As we have explained, the transaction will be legally binding once contracts have been exchanged. If you would like to discuss the matter or have any queries, we shall be pleased to arrange an appointment at a time convenient to you.

If you wish to proceed with the transaction please sign the contract where marked, and return all the documents to us together with your cheque drawn in our favour for the deposit of £...

We look forward to hearing from you.

P8 To vendor's solicitor enclosing contract and deposit

We now enclose the part of the contract signed by our client together with our cheque for the deposit of £..., to be held by you as stakeholder.

Please hold these to our order pending despatch by you to us of the part contract signed by the vendor.

P9 To building society/insurer regarding insurance of the property

Property ....
Borrower/Insured ....
Roll number/Reference.....................................

We confirm our telephone conversation of *(date)* informing you that contracts on the purchase have been exchanged, and request-

ing you to insure the property immediately under *(state type of policy required)* in the amount of £. . . . . .
(Request a proposal form if required. Check the terms regarding insurance if purchasing a lease. Check mortgagee's instructions.)

P10 To client confirming exchange of contracts

We are pleased to confirm that contracts have been exchanged for your purchase/lease of the property, with completion arranged for *(date)*, in accordance with your instructions. Insurance on the property in the sum of £. . . has been effected by *(name of Society or Insurer)* from the date of exchange when the risk passed to you.

We have now to investigate the vendor's title to the property, and will contact you again when the completion documents are ready for you to sign.

P11 To vendor's solicitor with requisitions on title

We enclose our requisitions on title and, subject to satisfactory replies thereto, a draft conveyance/assignment/transfer for your approval.

If you approve the transfer as drawn will you please retain the top copy as the engrossment. *(This will not apply if transfer has to be executed by the purchaser.)*

P12 To vendor's solicitor sending engrossed deed

Thank you for your letter of *(date)* returning the draft conveyance/assignment/transfer as approved. We now enclose the engrossment for execution by the vendor. *(If necessary this will have already been executed by the purchaser.)* Will you ensure that the plan is also signed. Please confirm the completion arrangements.

P13 To client regarding execution of the deed(s)

The documents have now been prepared in readiness for completion. We shall be pleased if you will contact us to arrange an appointment at a time convenient to you to obtain your signature and discuss the completion arrangements.

(If the matter has to be dealt with by post): We enclose the following documents for you to sign in readiness for completion. *(List all deeds and documents; explain the various clauses in the deed(s) as necessary and the purpose of each document. In dealing with the mortgage explain the legal effect and draw particular attention to the mortgagor's covenants.)*

Will you please sign the deed(s) where indicated, in the presence of an adult witness who is not a party to the deed, and who should then add his or her name, address, and occupation also where indicated; and also sign the documents not requiring a witness.

We take this opportunity of enclosing the completion statement and our bill of costs and disbursements for your approval. We shall be pleased to receive your cheque for £..., being the amount required to complete the purchase as shown on the statement, by *(date)* in order to clear this through our account before completion.

It will be helpful if you will return all of the signed deeds and documents to us as soon as possible.

P14 To building society with report on title and request for mortgage advance

Property ....
Borrower ....
Roll number ....

We have now investigated the vendor's title to the property and enclose our report. Completion has been arranged for *(date)* and we shall be pleased to receive your cheque for the advance by *(date)* in order to clear this through our account before completion.

(Check the Society's instructions, use any forms provided for this purpose, and enclose all documents required.)

P15 To insurer regarding assignment of policy for endowment mortgage

Life assured..
Policy number ....

We act for *(name of building society)* who are proposing to take an assignment of the above policy, and we shall be grateful if you will confirm that:

1. The policy is in full force and effect, and premiums have been paid to date.
2. Age is admitted.
3. You have received no notice of dealings relating to the policy, and your Company does not have a charge on the policy.

We shall in due course serve Notice of Assignment on you. If in the meantime you receive any Notices relating to the policy, we shall be grateful if you will note our interest and inform us accordingly.

P16 To vendor's solicitor completing by post

We enclose a banker's draft for £....., for the completion monies, and we thank you for your agreement to complete by post and to act as our agent.

We enclose the following *(list documents enclosed, eg counterpart lease, deposit release).*

(Give instructions as to any other agent. List deeds and documents required, including undertakings, receipts, authority addressed to tenant. List action required, including memorandum of sale to be endorsed on retained documents, abstract to be marked.)

Please arrange for the keys to be released to our client, and forward all deeds and documents to us without delay.

We are grateful for your assistance in this matter.

P17 To bank arranging credit transfer of completion money

Re: *(Name of client)*
     Purchase of *(address of property)*

Please effect an immediate telegraphic transfer of the amount of £..., from our client account no. ......, to *(name and branch address of vendor's solicitor's bank)* for credit to *(title and number of the account to be credited).*

Please debit your charge to our office account no.......

(It may be necessary to arrange the credit transfer with your bank by telephone and then confirm the instruction in a letter delivered by hand.)

P18 To building society confirming completion

Property ....
Borrower ....
Roll number ....
The purchase/lease and mortgage of the property were completed today as arranged and we enclose our completion report.

We are arranging for the conveyance/assignment/lease to be produced to the Stamp Office and we will register the borrower's title and the Society's mortgage with HM Land Registry. We will then forward the deeds and documents to you.

(Check the Society's instructions and use any forms provided for this purpose.)

P19 To insurer giving notice of assignment of life policy

Life assured..
Policy number ....
We thank you for the information contained in your letter of *(date)*

in reply to our previous enquiry *(see letter P15)*.

The mortgage of the life policy to *(name of building society)* has now been completed and we enclose Notice of Assignment in duplicate.

Will you please acknowledge receipt by signing and returning one copy of the Notice.

(Check the Society's mortgage instructions and use any form provided for this purpose. A printed form of notice of Assignment of Life Policy can be purchased from law stationers.)

P20 To lessor's solicitor giving notice of assignment/mortgage

Property ....
Date of Lease ....
Parties to Lease ....

We act for *(name of client)* on the assignment/mortgage of the above leasehold property. We understand that you act for the lessor *(name)* and in accordance with the requirements of the lease we enclose Notice of Assignment/Mortgage in duplicate, and a cheque for the prescribed fee of £....

Will you please acknowledge receipt by signing and returning one copy of the Notice.

(Check the covenants in the lease to ascertain the exact requirements. A printed form of Notice to Lessor can be purchased from law stationers.)

P21 To insurer of leasehold property giving notice of assignment/mortgage

Property insured..
Policy number ....

We act for *(name of client)* on the assignment of the lease of *(describe property)*.

Please arrange for the interest of our client, and of his mortgagee *(name)* for whom we also act, to be endorsed on the policy.

Please then provide us with a copy of the endorsement.

(Check the covenants in the lease and the lessor's policy to ascertain the exact requirements.)

P22 To client confirming completion

We are pleased to confirm that your purchase/lease of the property was completed today, as arranged. Your mortgage with the *(name of building society)* was also completed, and the Society will be contacting you with regard to the monthly payments, the first of which is due on *(date).*

We will now arrange for the conveyance/assignment/transfer/lease to be presented to the Stamp Office after which we shall register your title to the property with HM Land Registry. Once this has been completed the documents of title will be forwarded to your building society to hold as security for the loan.

(Ensure that client is provided with copies of documents needed for future reference, eg lease, restrictive covenants, mortgage and Society's rules.)

Appendix 3

List of conveyancing forms

The forms may be purchased from Fourmat Publishing and most law stationers.

* Indicates a special Fourmat number.

Contracts

*	F501	Contract for the sale of land by reference to either the National Conditions of Sale or The Law Society's Contract for Sale
	Con14	The National Conditions of Sale — with or without special conditions
		The Law Society's Contract for Sale 1984 edition (pink form)

Enquiries and Requisitions

*	F505	Preliminary enquiries
	Con 29	
	Long	Enquiries before contract
*	F510	Requisitions on title
	Con 28B	Requisitions on title
	Con 29A	Enquiries of District Councils (not London Boroughs)
	Con 29AX	Requisition for Enquiries of District Councils
	Con 29D	Enquiries of Local Authority — London Borough Councils or the Corporation of London
	Con 29DX	Requisition for Enquiries of Local Authority — London Borough Councils or the Corporation of London
	Con 29E	Request for a search in the register kept pursuant to s.79 of the Rent Act 1977

Assignments

*	F515	Assignment of National House-Building Council agreement
*	F520	Notice of assignment, charge or sub-lease

Land Registry forms under the Land Registration Acts 1925–1971

Applications to register dealings

A4	Whole of land in title
A5	Part of land in title

Assents

56	Assent or appropriation
57	Vesting assent (settled land)

Authority to inspect

* F600	Authority to inspect the register

Cautions

13 & 14	Application to register caution against first registration
16	Withdrawal of a caution against first registration
63 & 14	Caution against dealings with registered land
71	Withdrawal of a caution against dealings
100	Application for renewal of registration of a notice or caution (Land Registration (Matrimonial Homes) Rules 1983)

Charges

45A	Charge of whole
45B	Charge of part
45C	Charge accompanying a first registration
45D	Charge accompanying a transfer of part
53	Discharge of registered charge
53(Co)	Discharge of registered charge of which a company or corporation (including a building society) is the proprietor
54	Transfer of charge

Conversions

6	Application for conversion of title after 10 or 15 years on register
8	Application for conversion of title after less than 10 or 15 years on register

Credit account

105	Credit account voucher

Deposit of documents

A15	To await registration
A14	In connection with pending registration

First registrations

Application by solicitors for first registration on behalf of:

1B	a recent purchaser other than a company or corporation of freehold land
2B	a recent purchaser other than a company or corporation of leasehold land with good leasehold title
2F	a recent purchaser other than a company or corporation of leasehold land with absolute title
1E	a company or corporation, being a recent purchaser, of freehold land
2E	a company or corporation, being a recent purchaser, of leasehold land with good leasehold title
2 F(Co)	a company or corporation, being a recent purchaser, of leasehold land with absolute leasehold title
1C	an applicant other than a company or corporation, not a recent purchaser, of freehold land
2C	an applicant other than a company or corporation, not a recent purchaser, of leasehold land
1C (Co)	a company or corporation, not a recent purchaser, of freehold land
2C (Co)	a company or corporation, not a recent purchaser, of leasehold land
3B	an original lessee, not a company or corporation, with good leasehold title
3F	an original lessee, not a company or corporation, with absolute leasehold title
3E	an original lessee, being a company or corporation, with good leasehold title
3F (Co)	an original lessee, being a company or corporation, with absolute leasehold title

List of documents

A13	List of documents sent to HM Land Registry

Notices

17	Priority notice against first registration
84	Application to register notice of lease
85A	Notice of deposit of land or charge certificate
85B	Notice of intended deposit of land certificate on first registration
85C	Notice of intended deposit of land certificate on a dealing
86	Withdrawal of a notice of deposit or intended deposit of land certificate or charge certificate
99	Application for registration of a notice (Land Registration (Matrimonial Homes) Act 1983)
100	Application for renewal of registration of a notice or caution (Land Registration (Matrimonial Homes) Act 1983).

Office copies

A44	Application for office copies

Restrictions

75	Application to register a restriction
77	Application to withdraw a restriction

Searches

91	Application for information as to a notice of lease
94A	Application by purchaser for official search with priority in respect of the whole of land in a title
94B	Application by purchaser for official search with priority in respect of part of land in a title
94C	Application for official search without priority of the entries in the Register
96	Application for an official search of the index map
101	Application for certificate of inspection of filed plan
106	Application by mortgagee for official search (Land Registration (Matrimonial Homes) Rules 1983)

Transfers

19	Transfer of whole
19 draft	Draft transfer of whole
19 (Co)	Transfer of whole by company or corporation
19 (Co) draft	Draft transfer of whole by company or corporation
19JP	Transfer of whole to joint proprietors
19JP Draft	Draft transfer of whole to joint proprietors
19(R.72)	Transfer of whole under Rule 72
19(R.72) Draft	Draft transfer of whole under Rule 72
20	Transfer of part
20 Draft	Draft transfer of part
43	Transfer of part imposing fresh restrictive covenants
43 Draft	Draft transfer of part imposing fresh restrictive covenants

Transmission

82	Application to register the personal representatives of a deceased proprietor
83	Application to register death of joint proprietor

Land Charges Forms under the Land Charges Act 1972

Registration

K1	Application for registration of a land charge (except Class F)
K2	Application for registration of a land charge of Class F
K6	Application for registration of a priority notice

Renewal

K7   Application for the renewal of a registration (except
              Class F)
K8   Application for the renewal of a registration of a land
              charge of Class F

Rectification

K9   Application for rectification of an entry in the register

Continuation

K10   Continuation of an application

Cancellation

K11   Application for cancellation of an entry in the register
              (except Class F)
K13   Application for cancellation of a land charge of Class F

Declaration

K14   Declaration in support of an application for
              registration or rectification

Searches

K15   Application for an official search
K16   Application for an official search (bankruptcy only)

Office copies

K19   Application for an office copy of an entry in the register

Certificate of cancellation

K20   Application for a certificate of the cancellation of an
              entry in the register

Local Land Charges

LLC1   Requisition for search and official certificate of search

Commons Registration

CR21   Requisition for an official search (Register of Common
              Land/Town or Village Greens)

Fees and Duties

Conveyancing Fees & Duties, (Lawyers Costs & Fees Series No.5), Fourmat
Publishing. Includes Stamp Duties; Land Registry and Land Charges Fees;
recommended charges for building society advances; search fees.

Index